REFLECTIONS OF TIME

REFLECTIONS OF TIME

A COLLECTION

GILBERT HOLTS JR.

authorHOUSE®

AuthorHouse™
1663 Liberty Drive
Bloomington, IN 47403
www.authorhouse.com
Phone: 1-800-839-8640

Published by AuthorHouse   12/18/2012

ISBN: 978-1-4772-8755-2 (sc)
ISBN: 978-1-4772-8754-5 (e)

Library of Congress Control Number: 2012920824

Any people depicted in stock imagery provided by Thinkstock are models, and such images are being used for illustrative purposes only.
Certain stock imagery © Thinkstock.

This book is printed on acid-free paper.

Because of the dynamic nature of the Internet, any web addresses or links contained in this book may have changed since publication and may no longer be valid. The views expressed in this work are solely those of the author and do not necessarily reflect the views of the publisher, and the publisher hereby disclaims any responsibility for them.

For Japera,

The beauty of My Life.

For Jashé,

The Strength of my Life.

For Malachi,

The Virtue of My Life.

Together They Are,

The Love of My Life.

ACKNOWLEDGEMENTS

First and foremost I want to thank God for giving me the opportunity, mindset, and talent to put this book together. Next I want to thank everyone at Author House Publishing Company, especially Tim Murphy and Winona Reed who played a major part in making this project work. I want to thank my sister Angel for motivating and encouraging me to keep writing poetry. It was because of her that I started to keep all the poetry I've written and fueled my desire to get better. I want to thank Kit, one of my professors at Southeast Community and Technical College, for helping me fine tune my writing skills. He helped me find new and different ways of using a pencil and paper. I want to thank my grandmother/foster mother, Alberta Holts A.K.A Mother Holts, for instilling in me the fear and love of God and the knowledge that through Him anything is possible. I'd like to also thank Kami, Boss Man, Jay, Aunt Julia, and the late Markelle Pettygrue for their encouragement and undying support. I'd like to thank Kim Trotter for getting the ball rolling so that I could get this project started. I'd like to thank Uncle Ricky for the talks that we had in the garden up there on 2nd Street. He was always like a second father in giving me life changing advice, wisdom, and sharing with me his experience so that I wouldn't have to go through them. Last, but not least I want to thank my father, Gilbert Holts Sr., my younger brother Deion Holts, and my younger sister Kashia Holts, for all the time and energy they put into helping get this book ready for the publishing company.

CONTENTS

Introduction: Getting Started xi

Chapter 1: Reflections of My Mind..1

Chapter 2: Reflections of My Heart...78

Chapter 3: Reflections From: Me to You...119

Chapter 4: Reflections of My Life..151

Chapter 5: Reflections of My Faith 170

Chapter 6: R. I. P...211

In Remembrance of..228

GETTING STARTED

I have always been able to write poetry, but I really didn't get serious about it until I attended college with my older sister Angel in 2005. Before then I would only write a little here and there; maybe for someone's funeral, church anniversary, a holiday, or just to make someone smile. Sometimes I would enter poetry in contests at school and online just to see how I would do. Those that I would let read my poetry, would tell me that I had a talent for writing; but to me, it seemed like something anybody could do. My sister would tell me how it would amaze her to see how easily I could write poems. I find it a lot easier to express myself when I write; if I write it in the form of a poem. Honestly, now that I think about it, I started writing real heavy in 2002; after the death of one of my childhood friends, Lil Rut. I guess you can say that pain is the fuel for my poetry.

It was Angel who encouraged me to keep writing poetry and to try to do something with them. Also, it was originally her idea for me to put them all in a book and have them published. I really didn't know how to get started on getting an actual book published, so I just kept putting it off for a long time. It wasn't until six years later that Kim, a friend of the family, was able to find the contact information of Author House Publishing Company to get the ball rolling. After my dad and younger brother set everything up, all I had to do was just put the book in order. After completing that task, all that was left to do was to think of a name for the book. That's when I decided to name the book "Reflections of Time". I chose that title because every poem in this book reflects back on a certain personal experience, how I felt during a certain situation, and certain time periods of my life.

I divided all the poems into six chapters and each poem has the original date in which it was written. In each chapter the poems are placed in order from earliest date to the latest. That way you'll be able to see the growth I've experienced, in each area, on my long and continuous journey during my life so far. The first and longest chapter is called "Reflections of My Mind". All the poems in this chapter are things that have been on my mind a time or two, or just expressing how I feel or felt about a certain subject or situation. Whenever I have something on my mind, and it's been bothering me, I write a poem about it and it makes me feel a lot better. Writing poems about my feelings or problems seem, for me, the equivalent of opening up and talking to someone about them. The second chapter is called "Reflections of My Heart" and this is the love chapter of my life. Sometimes when I want to say something to a female that I don't have the nerve to say to her face, I just write a poem. Most of the time I just keep the poem in my notebook, and at other times I may give them a copy of the poem that I write. There have only been three females that have had a special place in my heart over the years. I've had feelings for a lot of females but there are only three that could have my all at any time. Out of those three, only one holds and may always hold that number one spot in my life (second to Jesus of course). She knows who she is . . . "we still see you hatas in our rear view mirror, so leave us alone". I hope you got that.

The third chapter is called "Reflections From: Me To: You" and this chapter includes letters that I've written to people for various reasons. The fourth chapter is called "Reflections of My Life", and these poems tell a little bit about the major periods in my life. Even though it is the shortest chapter, I believe it says the most about what I've been through. The Fifth chapter is called "Reflections of My Faith", and this chapter is full of religious poetry. I've written one or two previously throughout my writing journey, but since I've submitted my life to the Lord in May 2011, I've written more than I ever have before. The sixth chapter is called "R.I.P", and this chapter includes some poems I've written about some of the people I've lost in my life. The last section of my book is called "In Remembrance Of", and this page is a list of all the special people that I've lost in my lifetime thus far. They will always truly be missed.

I hope that as the reader, you enjoy every bit of what you read. I had you all in mind the whole time I was putting this book together. I hope that you are able to read and understand each poem with the seriousness and open-mindedness that I had when I wrote them. Thank you for your support and May God bless you, and keep me in your prayers.

<u>Chapter 1</u>

REFLECTIONS

OF  MY

MIND

"A Face besides My Own"

When I look into a mirror
I see a face besides my own,
Compared to some a face of a boy
but a face that's fully grown.

A face that never smiles
because it's where I hide my pain,
No sign of being happy or being sad
the expression is always plain.

It's almost like a mask
that nobody sees but me,
A mask that's never worn
I have to draw it for you to see.

This face, it tells a story
a story that very few know,
That's why it has no eyes
so the story it cannot show.

When you take a look at the face
look carefully at each part,
Three parts that stand for something special
three parts I hold close to my heart.

The eyes on top represent me
because I am the oldest,
The mouth represents my brother
because he is the boldest.

The nose represents my sister
in the middle is where she dwells,
Even though she's represented by the nose
she's the one who always tells.

For as long as I can remember
this face has been my mark of trade.
No matter where I chose to put it
in my heart is where it stayed.

Now you know why I draw the face
and why in my reflection it's this I see,
It reminds me of my brother and sister
who are both a big part of me.

"Standing Still"

3 April 2003

You say that you're listening
but you aint heard nothing,
Then when asked a question
you do nothing but cussing.

They say beauty lies
in the eyes of the beholder,
But beauty really lies
in the head on your shoulders.

You talk real fast
but you move real slow,
There's some stuff about a brother
that you just don't know.

You go get your guns
and all that stuff,
But it all won't matter
when that hour gets rough.

Just keep your mouth shut
and try to keep it real,
Cause it's a man like me
you really don't want to feel.

Do whatever you do
and say whatever you say,
Just don't say nothing about me
because I don't like to play.

I send them real hard
and they come real quick,
I'll be the last one standing
the only one holding the stick.

Y'all supposed to be starting
but y'all sitting on the bench,
Playing behind the super man
from a small town called Lynch.

My life is full of heartaches
and a lot of pain,
But I'm still that super man
driving the only train.

I hope you are listening
to these words that I speak
Because you'll never catch me slipping
even if a brother is sleep.

"It's Good"

9 December 2003

It's good to laugh
to laugh and smile,
Especially with someone you love
because it makes it worthwhile.

It's good to talk
to talk about everything,
Especially with someone you love
because that's what makes your heart sing.

It's good to play
To play around with your son
Especially with my . . .
excuse me I don't have one.

It's good to cry
to cry tears of joy,
Especially on that first Christmas
when a son received his first toy.

It's good to love
to love unconditionally,
Especially when it's your friends
but in my life it's not a reality

It's good to dream
to dream about future plans.
Even if the woman you discuss it with
doesn't want you as her man.

It's good to have high hopes
high hopes about making it big,
Even if the girl you want to take
snaps your heart in two like a twig.

It's good to have a family that loves you
but there's nothing like your own,
A wife, some kids, and a dog
and a house to call your own.

"A Cry For Help"

9 February 2004

I've been trying to keep it real with my family man,
but the world is getting weirder, people changing lanes.

People all up in my face they trying to get me man,
I aint the one to fall weak they don't understand.

Daddy Bill is really gone still can't believe it man,
and my thoughts is getting shaky will you help me man.

Need some guidance need some hope like you aint to blame,
and everything will get better you just have to wait.

My thoughts are altered man now tell me who's to blame,
I know that things will get better but they still the same.

I dream about the past and the future man,
but in my dreams there's some things I don't understand.

My life is full of rainy days wish you can see 'em man,
but if you seen, you probably still wouldn't understand.

My only son died a big secret man,
waking up every day feeling nothing but pain.

I really love my momma but she hurt me man,
I made a promise to myself it'll never happen again.

Daddy kept me safe while momma tried to do me wrong,
can you see that I'm hurting that's why I wrote this song.

People I see every day be trying to judge me man,
but it's some stuff about this man they don't understand.

And my friends they starting to treat me a little different man,
so my heart is where I really feel most of my pain.

I try to talk to people but it hurts to bad,
and when I do talk about it I start feeling sad.

So I'd rather hold it and think about other thangs,
and live my life day to day praying for a change.

May not be the way to live but it's all I know,
until something puts me back on that narrow road.

It's true
All my people know the pain that I done been through
All my life been struggling, hurting, and trying to find the truth
Everybody trying to tell me things that I should do
And they say Gilbert don't you worry cause we will do it with you.

"Time"

A misjudgment of time
a mistake often made,
No corrections or no take backs
I'm sorry it's just too late.

Once time is lost
you can't get it back,
You have to manage time well
but that's what some lack.

With time comes new life
at times also death,
Time is very precious
so never just hold your breath.

With time comes hope
and a lot of understanding,
Therefore with time comes wisdom
and wisdom makes good commanding.

Always keep track
and take into consideration,
That time brings wisdom
but you must have patience.

"Without"

16 September 2006

Life without pain
stress and confusion,
Life without hatred
and parents abusing.

Life without notes
rhythm and music
Life without drugs
and those that abuse it.

Life without patience
time and free will,
Life without gangs
and niggas packing steel.

Life without dreams
motivation and hope,
Life without disappointment
and people telling you no.

Life with goals
progress and achievement,
Life without racism
and people who believe it.

Life without power
money and cars,
Life without the moon
the sun and the stars.

Life without me
you and our friends,
Life without all of us
meeting our end.

Life without ignorance
fear and complications,
Life without contradiction
and the people who be hatin'.

Life without honor
morals and respect,
Life without love
and all that you'd expect.

Life without pictures
short stories and poems,
Life without artist's
and the people who know 'em.

"Reasons To Live"

19 October 2006

Growing older I am
In a world all alone,
Life's really taking its toll
But still I'm like a bone.
Each moment that passes
Reality seems to bite,
Trials and tribulations
Damn it isn't right.
Everyone has a reason for
Quitting and losing control,
Unique qualities I do possess
And now it's this you know.
Understanding me is a test
Not many are able to pass,
Unless you're willing to study
Charm won't make it last.
Can you accept this challenge
And can you follow my trail,
Really it is worth it
Don't try and you'll never fail.
In time good things will come
Happy wishes will soon follow,
Of all the things there are
Love is the hardest to swallow.
True love is something special
So is the life that gives,
Just remember to cherish it all
Reasons for us to live

"One and Then Some"

15 December 2006

One often meets his destiny
on the road he took to avoid it,
One often meets his end
in the beginning and that's bull shit.

Some often remember situations
that never really occurred,
Exactly how they said
that's why the picture is blurred.

One often remembers love
as something that causes pain,
One often remembers her
which is love, they are the same.

Some say that problems are
the product of our ignorance,
Some say they can't be solved
even if they go the distance.

One often remembers humility
the way it stared him in the face,
One often remembers you
the time you brought me to that place.

Some often refer to beauty
as something you rarely see,
While I refer to beauty
As her being here with me.

One loves to see you smile
especially when he's the cause,
One loves it when you're around
in his world you have no flaws.

Some say she's not the one
but yet I truly differ,
If life was like a boat
then truly I'd be the skipper.

"Do You Know What Its Like"

3 February 2007

Do you know what it's like
to be nowhere all the time,
Not meaning a deserted place
but being alone in your mind.

Do you know what it's like
to be nowhere when you try,
Try to find a certain someone
but you can't so you just cry.

Do you know what it's like
to be nowhere even when,
Even when you've just started
and your journey you now begin.

Do you know what it's like
to be nowhere when you fall,
Can't even cry for help
because there's no one there to call

Do you know what it's like
to be nowhere when you cry,
And you can't find any comfort
no matter how hard you try.

Do you know what it's like
to be nowhere even though,
You know how to read a map
but only a half is what you hold.

Do you know what it's like
to really be deeply in love,
But when you reach for a kiss
all you get is just a shove.

Do you know what it's like
to always know the truth,
Even when you don't want to see it
it seems to always grab for you.

Do you know what it's like
when you're trying to maintain,
But really it's hard to do
when you're constantly feeling pain.

Do you know what it's like
to always see her lies,
And constantly within yourself
you're always asking why.

"Feeling Me"

18 November 2007

Alone in this world
I always seem to be,
Many people
Many problems
Many fingers pointing at me.

Really a good person
just a little misunderstood,
Full of anger
Full of pain
Full of reasons why I should.

Only if I knew
back then what I know now,
I wouldn't watch
I wouldn't listen
I wouldn't let him show me how.

Pain is a feeling
that I've felt for many years,
I've gained
I've lost
I've cried a lot of tears.

Reasons for my actions
I try to explain,
No excuses
No mistakes
Just me in every way.

Emotions and my mind
running wild no control,
Only pain
Only sorrow
Only me being alone.

Please don't pity me
or feel sorry not at all,
My heart
My weakness
My reasons for standing tall.

Blessings all the time
and I hope they never stop,
My life
My family
My friends are they not.

Understanding in a way
I journey to succeed,
No doubt
No failure
Just you believing me.

Once in my life
I've experienced tranquility,
No sleep
No friends
Not even family.

People in my life
I try to keep them close,
My feelings
My love
My heart they will know.

Every time that I think
about the things that I lost,
My son
My momma
My friends at what cost.

Life has it's own
it's way of letting us know,
Negative people
Negative talk
Negative feelings let them go.

Knowledge that I've gained
and experience I try to share,
Only you
Only me
The only two that really care.

Only if you can
my shoes try to fill,
With family
With life
With friends I keep it real.

Problems if you have them
I can help you get through,
Nothing more
Nothing less
Nothing at all but the truth.

Reasons just listen
and try to understand,
My time
My struggle
My journey to be a man.

Understanding is a gift
that I've had for a while,
Many souls
Many minds
Many faces I've made smile.

Talk if not to me
to someone else at least try,
Let 'em see
Let 'em feel
Let 'em know why you cry.

Cries I can hear 'em
too many voices help me out,
Now you know
Now you see
What lil' Gilbert's all about.

"Helping Out"

19 November 2007

Reality has its own way
it's own way of letting us know,
The people we should keep in our lives
and the ones we should let go.

Most of us we listen
and watch for signs to come,
While the rest sit back and hear nothing
and their mouths they're quick to run.

I was told once before
good things come to those with patience,
If this statement is really true
then why am I still waitin'.

If good things come to those with patience
then why haven't I received,
I really don't understand it
maybe it doesn't pertain to me.

Life has taken its toll
on me, for real it has,
So much pain built up inside
so my smiles are now a mask

The mask that hides the anger
is the same that hides my pain,
It's also the one that hides
the feeling of me being shamed.

23

I always try to help
but never some more than others,
With the thought in mind that everyone
should be equally considered as brothers.

Not knowing the situation
I jumped in head first,
Trying to help so many people
my own life I may have cursed.

My father always told me
that my mouth would get me in trouble,
But never once did he say
that my heart could make it double.

At times I close my eyes
and wish I was never here,
Frustrated by my decisions
and the pain pushes out the tears.

"A Baby Story"

24 November 2007

What in the hell is going on
and who is making all that noise,
Where did all these kids come from
and where in the hell did they get those toys.

That's how the dream starts off
and then I start playing with the kids,
Then I hear this baby crying
and notice that cry sounds just like his.

Now I'm looking everywhere
but still I cannot find,
Find where the cry is coming from
but I know that baby's mine.

All of a sudden the room gets quiet
there's nobody else there but me,
In an instant I'm holding my son
now I'm wondering how this could be.

By this time I start crying
and I hold him close to my heart,
I know it's just a dream,
but I'm wishing we never part.

I started to look at his face
as I pulled him from my chest,
That's when I noticed my son is dead
so I guess you know the rest.

This dream has haunted my sleep
for now quite some time,
To really be exact
it has been since ninety-nine.

I miss my little boy
for real I'm telling you,
I just wish I can stop having this dream
but I don't know what to do.

"Step Into My World"

12 December 2007

Come step into my world

and understand the things that I see,

Understand my reasons for living

and the reason why I am me.

Come step into my world

and understand the things that I hear,

Understand my reasons for living

and the reason I live in fear.

Come step into my world

and understand the things that I say,

Understand my reasons for living

and the reason I went my own way.

.

Come step into my world

and understand the things that I do,

Understand my reasons for living

and the reason I do it to you.

Come step into my world

and understand the things that I keep,

Understand my reasons for living

and the reason why I can't sleep.

Come step into my world

and understand the things that I know,

Understand my reasons for living

and the reason why I should show.

Come step into my world
And understand the things that I give,
Understand my reason for living
And the reason I want to live.

Come step into my world
and understand the things that I don't,
Understand my reasons for living
and the reason why I won't.

Come step into my world
and understand the thing that I need,
Understand my reasons for living
and the reason why I smoke weed.

Come step in to my world
and understand the things that I think,
Understand my reasons for living
and the reason why I drink.

Come step into my world
and understand the things that I caught,
Understand my reasons for living
and the reason why they can't be bought.

Come step into my world
and understand the things that I face,
Understand my reason for living
and the reason why I need my space.

"The Little Boy"

6 March 2008

Come help the little boy
that's trapped inside a man,
A man full of hurt
no one seems to understand.

Come help the little boy
that's always feeling pain,
Who helps the little boy
when its help he's trying to gain

Come help the little boy
that always has something to say,
But who hears the little boy
when they're turned the other way.

Come feel for the little boy
that's lost most of his friends,
Will you feel for the little boy
when the time comes for his to end.

Come play with the little boy
who wants to come outside,
Will you play with the little boy
when it's feelings he wants to hide.

Come stand with the little boy
who seems to have no home,
Will you stand with the little boy
even when he stands alone.

Come eat with the little boy
who doesn't have a meal,
Will you hate the little boy
if it's yours he's trying to steal.

Come talk to the little boy
who hasn't said a word,
Will you hear the little boy
when his voice is trying to be heard.

Come comfort the little boy
who cries in his sleep,
Will you comfort the little boy
even if that boy is me.

"I Wish I Could Have Been There"

18 May 2008

I wish I could have been there
to watch Moses part the Red Sea,
If I lived back in that time
I wonder if God would talk to me.

I wish I could have been there
to meet with Dr. King,
To listen to one of his sermons
and to hear his choir sing.

I wish I could have been there
to watch Rosa take her seat,
Maybe if I was on that bus
she would have sat next to me.

I wish I could have been there
the day Malcolm gave his last speech,
To warn him about his future
but would he have listened to me.

I wish I could have been there
to stop them from ever dating,
Maybe if I could have stopped them
her actions I wouldn't be hating.

I wish I could have been there
before Angel took his hand,
So very hard I would have tried
to introduce a better man.

I wish I could have been there
three days before he turned three,
I believe if I could have been there
my son would have been with me.

I wish I could have been there
the night Lil Rut had died,
To convince him not to go to the club
so hard I would have tried.

I wish I could have been there
at least an hour before Daddy Bill passed,
To tell him how much I love him
and how that love would always last

"Motivated"

12 June 2008

I'm motivated to quit doing
the things that I use to do,
I have a beautiful baby boy
and to him I'm going to be true.

I'm motivated to quit playing
this game that I use to play,
I have a beautiful baby boy
and I don't want to go away.

I'm motivated to quit seeing
The things that I use to see,
I have a beautiful baby boy
who's going to want to be like me.

I'm motivated to quit thinking
the things that I use to think,
I have a beautiful baby boy
my mentality changed in a wink.

I'm motivated to quit saying
the things that I use to say,
I have a beautiful baby boy
to me attention he is going to pay.

I'm motivated to handle
the things that I need to handle,
I have a beautiful baby boy
and his life I don't want to dismantle.

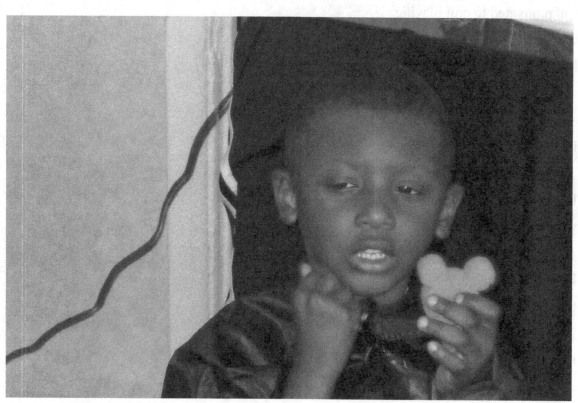

"You All I'll Keep Close"

18 July 2003

Some people listen
and others talk
My path in life
pray you don't walk.

I've been battling with life
for a long twenty-two years
I've had a lot of fun
but I've cried more tears

I often pray for
good times to come fast,
Because you'll never know
which day could be your last.

My day is coming
but I don't know when,
I just hope when it does
my soul is free of sin.

I wish you could walk
in my footsteps of pain,
Then you'll see why
I seem crazy or insane.

I lost something special
and he was a part of me,
He was my only son
and he was only three.

Since I lost my mother
all I have is my father,
Oh she's alive and well
but with me she doesn't bother.

I've lost a lot of things
that really meant a lot to me,
But whatever I lose
will come back times three.

My heart is fragile
but my mind is strong,
This life that I live
I know that it's wrong.

One day I'll change
and I hope it won't be too late,
Because the price of my sins
I can't afford to pay.

I've done a lot of wrong
and I've done a lot of good,
I've misled a lot of people
a lot of people I've misunderstood.

I've finished this poem
and I did not cry,
I just hope my soul
Is free before I die.

"My Little Brother"

17 June 2008

On September the fourth
back in nineteen eighty-three
Yauntia came into this world
A little brother sent to me.

As a child he always tried
to be like his bigger bro,
But in time he would be better
which was something he didn't know.

Over time this boy grew up
and started making a name for himself,
The older he got the more trouble he was in
but daddy was always there to help.

He played for a D-1 school
at UK that boy was the man,
Out of all the people that watched him
me and daddy were his number one fans.

All through life that boy stayed strong
and always handle his biz,
But most importantly he was always there
to be a father to all of his kids.

"I Was Thinking"

18 July 2008

I was thinking the other day
and I told myself again,
It never fails for me in life
to always lose a friend.

Then I thought about my odds
the cards I've been dealt in life,
Even though there's no excuse
it wasn't fair it still wasn't right.

I then thought about religion
I was thinking about mine,
I've had twenty seven years
and still I'm way behind.

I thought about the ones I've lost
and the many tears that I have cried,
They always said it would get a lot better
but so far they all have lied.

I thought about my sister Angel
and then about her kids,
I thought about the love she has
and for them stuff she did.

I thought about my little boy
and how he has his daddy's eyes,
I made a promise to myself
to not tell him any lies.

I thought about my younger brother
and the stuff he's overcame,
And then I thought about our childhood
besides momma is it me that he blames.

I thought about my past relationships
and how they never seem to last,
All because I'm taken for granted
she tried to make me look like an ass.

I thought about my grandmother
we call her Mother Holts,
I thought about her closeness to God
I bet He rarely tells her no.

I thought about my father
he really did a good job,
He raised three kids and did it well
regardless of all the probs'.

"I Apologize"

(Verse 1)   June 2009

Every morning I wake up
with the same thought,
Thinking about my life
and the things that I done lost.

I think about mistakes that I have made
and at what cost,
I think about the season
that I chose to be the boss.

I think about my people
that's always feeling pain,
I think about the ones
that couldn't make it, went insane.

I think about the army
and how I got away
I think about my God
the reason why I pray.

This life I'm trying to live
it's got me losing patience
And one of my niggas just opened a book
He's reading revelations.

We trying to make this journey
because we all still waiting,
Don't think we going to make it
because of a man we call Satan.

41

You see this life I'm living
sometimes it makes me cry
The look on mammas face
I know she wants to ask me why

To stop the bad and better myself
so hard I'm gonna try
But if I fail I want you to know
that I apologize

[Hook]
All my life I apologize for the things I did,
All my life I apologize for the bull shit.
All my life I apologize for what it's worth
All my life I apologize on this verse.

"I Apologize"

(Verse 2)   15 June 2009

Every morning I wake up
Feeling the same pain,
Thinking about the reasons
Why I chose to run away.

I think about my momma
And how I was afraid,
I think about my daddy
And how he kept me safe.

I think about my sister
And how she almost died,
I think about the way I felt
As I began to cry.

I think about my brother
And still I wonder why,
I think about this past
And why he'd even try.

This life I'm trying to live
It's got me going crazy,
And every time that I open my phone
I'm staring at my baby.

I'm trying to make this journey
Because I know you still waiting,
Don't think I'm going to make it
Because of a thing we call patience.

You see this life I'm living
sometimes it makes me cry,
The look on daddy's face
I know he wants to ask me why.

To stop the bad and better myself
so hard I'm going to try,
But if I can't I want you to know
that I apologize.

[Hook]
All my life I apologize for the things I did,
All my life I apologize for the bull shit.
All my life I apologize for what it's worth,
All my life I apologize on this verse.

"I Apologize"

(Verse 3)   15 June 2009

Every night when I lay down
before I close my eyes,
I think about the people I lost
and then I start to cry.

To keep it out of my mind
so very hard I really try,
But I just can't stop
wondering why they had to die.

Somebody way back told me
told me about myself,
And after they heard my problems
they say I needed help.

That for the things I did
I should have been in jail,
They say that when He judge me
He gone send me to hell.

I really don't understand it
the things that people say,
I really don't want to play them
the games they tryin' to play.

I really don't want to go there
to the place they tryin' to stay,
I really don't want to eat it
the cake they trying to bake.

I'm just another nigga
out her strugglin' to make it
I keep it real with my niggas
I don't have to fake it.

Your finger in my face
get it out before I break it
Your life in my hands
snatch it out before I take it.

[Hook]
All my life I apologize for the things I did,
All my life I apologize for the bull shit.
All my life I apologize for what its worth,
All my life I apologize for this verse.

"Constant Wishing"

4 July 2009

I often ask myself
how I got in this situation,
Struggling so far away from home
because of my lack of patience.

Now I'm trying to find myself
and I need to do it fast,
The reason I moved so far from home
was to get away from my past.

Somebody told me before
about the happiness I wanted to see,
They said I'd never find it
until I looked inside of me.

Now how could I want something so much
but that something I already have,
So confused I often stay
but the thought it makes me laugh.

So I took a three day journey
with intentions of trying to succeed,
I just wanted a better life
and for my son to be with me.

Even though I don't admit it
I'm always thinking about my momma,
And I wish I could have her back
regardless of the pain and all her drama.

47

I'm trying to understand me
even for me it's hard to do,
Because no matter how hard I try
I just can't tell me the truth.

Mo. Holts would always tell me
that God was all I need,
And when things seem to get hard and rough
close my eyes and hit my knees.

I've never been at a point
where I've had to sleep inside my car,
Not because I have nowhere to go
but because home is just too far.

Mo. Holts tried to warn me
but for some reason I didn't listen,
And because of my lack of patience and reasoning
I'm in a state of constant wishing.

"If's On My Mind"

16 February 2011

If a tree falls in the forest
and there's no one around to hear it,
Does it really make a sound
even if nobody's near it.

If a person loses composure
in the midst of a group of people,
Does that in itself make them weak
and if so will there be a sequel.

If a baby cries for its mother
buts she's not around to hear,
Why does the baby continue to cry
without even shedding a tear.

If a man strays off the path
on his way to a destination,
Why does he get so upset
and ends up losing patience.

If a girl says that she loves you
and says it's from the heart,
Then why would she question a simple task
intending to keep us apart.

If a bird falls out of a tree
and finds it's place on the ground,
Why doesn't the mother go get it
forever lost never to be found.

If a father loses his son
but no one knows his secret,
Will he try to shed a tear
or does he try to keep it.

If a mother mistreats her son
and love is seldomly shown,
Is he really the one to blame
for the relationships that he's blown.

If a woman, most of her life
has been dealing with bad men,
How come when a good one comes around
she throws him back up in the wind.

If a person says they're real
and claims to be telling the truth,
How come when I catch there lies
my feelings react like a mute.

"Still Thinking"

18 April 2011

I was thinking the other day
about something I'd did in my past,
I try to keep in out of my head
but without effort it doesn't last.

I think a lot about my life
and how I may never get to be free,
I think about all those fingers
and how they're always pointed at me.

I thought about that night
and the reason for my actions,
Then I thought about a friend
giving me up for his satisfaction.

I think about my position
and I'm reminded of a game of chess,
I think about my next move
and how it brings me so much stress.

I thought about his family
and how I caused them so much pain,
Then I thought about her family
how with them I did the same.

I think about the truth
and what I'm trying to attain,
I think about the lie
and how it could take away the blame.

I thought about it more than once
and when I did I began to cry,
Then I thought about spending eternity
in hell if I tried to lie.

I think about all these people
and how some I used to fear,
I think about having no help
and how I'd always shed a tear.

I thought about Jashe' and Japera
and how I might not see them again,
Then I thought about Little Foot Jenkins
my son seeing daddy in the pen.

I think about all my talents
and why I never really tried to use them,
I think about my body and feelings
and how Corrina use to abuse them.

"If They Only Knew"

20 April 2011

If they only knew Corrina
and the way she used to beat me,
I'd bet they'd change their thoughts
and the way that they all treat me.

If they only knew about my downs
and how they outnumbered my ups,
They'd see why when people are thirsty
I'd always try to fill their cups.

If they only knew about Deion
and the things he's overcame,
I'd bet then they'd look at him different
and for his outcome he wouldn't be to blame.

If they only knew about Kashia
and how close she's came to death,
After hearing just a piece of her story
everybody would be holding their breath.

If they only knew Big Gilbert
and the opportunities he let pass by,
After knowing his kids was the reason
I'd bet never again they'd ask him why

If they only knew about Angel
and the trials she had to endure,
I'd bet when people heard her story
her perseverance would be their cure.

If they only knew about Mo. Holts
and how to God she'd always pray,
I'd bet if you took time and listened
you'd learn something new about faith.

If they only knew about Ricky
and how God did touch his life,
You'd know why he was blessed with wisdom
A new mind and a loving wife.

If they only knew the real me
and why I feel so much pain,
They'd know why most of my life
on me it always seems to rain.

"Maybe"

1 September 2011

Maybe I should go
to prison for a long time,
Or maybe I'm wrong though
and just only do half the time.

Maybe I don't know
and really I'm just trippin',
Or maybe I'm right though
and they just aint listenin'.

Maybe they do love
and really I'm just to scarred,
Or maybe I'm wrong though
and I'm really trying too hard.

Maybe I don't know
and really it's all in my head,
Or maybe I'm right though
and as a father to them I'm dead.

Maybe they do know
and really they're just too hurt,
Or maybe I'm wrong though
and they want to put me in the dirt.

Maybe I don't know
and I'm feeling this alone,
Or maybe I'm right though
and they want to hear me groan.

Maybe I should have told her
the truth about how I felt,
Or maybe I'm wrong though
and a bad hand is what I was dealt.

Maybe I don't know
and was scared to claim what could have been mine,
Or maybe I'm right though
and I'll know for sure in due time.

Maybe I'm just thinking
to hard about my past,
Or maybe I'm wrong though
and messed up to come in last.

Maybe I don't know
and just need to continue to pray
Or maybe I'm right though
and the way things are is where they'll stay.

"Periods of Time"

13 September 2011

One time I use to be happy
two times I almost quit,
Quit trying to be the person
I should have been to start wit'.

Three times I made that journey
four times I ended up lost,
To lost to keep going forward
so those journeys for me it cost.

Five times I've seen him cry
six times he's seen my eyes,
To late to take it all back
to late to stop their cries.

Seven times I just lost count
eight times I really tried,
They said that it could be done
and so far they all have lied.

Nine times I tried to reach her
ten times I tried to pray,
I always try to hear it
but I guess there's nothing to say.

Eleven hours it took to find it
twelve hours it took to see,
It really did take that long
for them to get to know me.

Thirteen days it was on my mind
the fourteenth I got it off,
What I said went to the wrong people
and it spread just like a cough.

Fifteen weeks I was getting depressed
the sixteenth I was all the way in,
It's never happened to me before
but in that state I know I can't win.

Seventeen months I had finished the mission
on the eighteenth I was fully aware,
Not many people know what happened
and on the real I still don't care.

Nineteen years I thought about going
now it's twenty they're trying to take,
They're not even trying to see
that it really was just a mistake.

"Trying Not To Lose Control"

19 September 2011

It's like no matter what I do
I can't get the pain to stop,
No matter how hard I seem to try
the balloon still tries to pop.

At times I really need to be alone
somewhere off just by myself,
And I really hate being around these spirits
I want to knock things off the shelf.

I have nobody to talk to
and I feel that no one cares,
I'm losing control of my anger
the same way that I'm losing my hairs.

Times like this I can honestly see
that Corrina did hurt me bad,
Anytime that I'm being pushed around
I hurt someone which is real sad.

It really takes a lot of effort
to try and control that emotion,
Regardless of what I'm doing
keeping control is my major devotion.

I wonder if I'm really crazy
or if I've experienced too much pain,
Because sometimes I get so angry
that it nearly drives me insane.

I get tired of turning the other check
in my case flipping the page,
I don't know how long I can do it
how long I can control my rage.

Keep praying, keep fasting, keep praising
that's what they tell me to do,
But I'd wonder if they would do it
only if they had to put on one shoe.

God knows that I am trying
but this war is getting real tough,
I don't know how much I can take
I don't know when it's going to be enough.

I can't just make you a promise
but I'm going to hold on the best way I can,
Please help me keep control of my emotions
and don't let the devil tear down this man.

"Pictures On A Wall"

6 November 2011

Sometimes I take walks in my mind
to get away from a stressful day,
Never really knowing where I'm headed
just letting my need to lead the way.

Sometimes I go to a place with
these pictures all over a wall,
Pictures of me watching my little boy
in my apartment on the floor trying to crawl.

Pictures of Jashe' and Japera
dancing in the middle of the streets,
A picture of Jashe' wearing a hat
dancing to one of my beats.

A picture of Japera laughing and
talking like she can really speak Spanish,
And a picture of Mother Holts telling
Kashia to quit acting so mannish.

I remember seeing a picture of daddy
smiling as big as he could,
When I first came home from the army
in my uniform asking "what's good".

I'll never forget the picture of Deion
after his first year playing with U.K.,
Holding an award with his daughter Camil
I just knew that he was on his way.

61

There are pictures of me looking down
with a sad look on my face,
In the same pictures I can see Angel
telling me that I can still win the race.

I see pictures of me and Angel falling
face down because we were slack,
In the same pictures I see Mother Holts
with a smile carrying us on her back.

Now these pictures are like one big collage
dating back since me and Angel was a kid,
Mother Holts carrying us on her back
teaching us the word is what she did.

At the end of the wall I see a blank picture
with the words that says future untold,
Under the pictures I see a label that reads
you can't see unless God unfolds.

"I'd Go Back To"

30 November 2011

I wish that I could rewind time
just to undo some of the past,
To right the wrongs that I could
and get rid of the pain that lasts.

I'd first go back to that night
that I went to go holla at Crow,
When Tony asked if I wanted him to take me
plain and simply I would have said "no".

I'd then go back to the day
that I decided to be done with the Army,
I would have never made that decision
but I was scared that the war would harm me.

I'd try to go back to the night
that Malachi had been conceived,
Before I ended up having a child
there were some things I should've achieved.

I'd really want to go back
to stop daddy from making her cry
Because she took it out on the three of us
and I still don't understand why.

I'd go back to the apartment I had
when I lived in number five,
I'd tell 'Kelle he could stay when he wanted
and then maybe he'd still be alive.

I'd go back to when he first got sick
when I'd help get him up and then sit back down,
I would have spent more time with Daddy Bill
and in '03 I would have never left town.

I'd go back to the time when I
was in school living at home,
Because of the guilt that I still feel
I would've never left the other two alone.

I'd go back to the very first time
I seen the man that drove the eighty-eight,
I'd try my best to keep them apart
in order to wipe clean her slate.

Sometimes I wish I'd never been born
and honestly I really do mean it,
I pray that Christ takes hold of my life
and with His blood decides to clean it.

"Situations"

18 March 2012

The cards that I've been dealt
in life don't seem fair,
So the way I played my hand
was foolish and full of despair.

When I tried to play them straight
I was blinded by an awful glare,
So most of my life I played
the game not even being aware.

Being aware of all the demons
that stood right there in front of me,
In the form of drugs, in the form of friends
even in the form of family.

Trying to do the best they could
to keep me from ever trying to complete,
To complete the mission of knowing
and truly finding the God in me.

Disappointing the people I love
with every step I tried to take,
Blinded by the lack of knowledge
and ignorant decisions I'd try to make.

Trying to show the others that I
was real and how I wasn't fake,
But the whole time I'm a sinking boat
and the world is one big lake.

At night I lay in my cell doing
what I can trying not to cry,
Thinking about my son and all
the time that could possibly pass us by.

Got to make this journey even though
it's hard still going to have to try,
Try to figure out how to deal with the pain
I feel when I close my eyes.

All my life I've constantly
dealt with scary situations,
I do what I can to keep my head
and not lose my patience.

Never underestimating any of
the problems that I be facing,
Taking it day by day and praying
that they don't drive me crazy.

"I Think About"

(Verse 1)   23 March 2012

I think about my life
and what I've done with it,
I think about the people I met
and where I chose to sit.

I think about my future
and what it holds for me,
I think about the plans I've had
and about the number three.

I think about my son
and the good times that we had,
I think about his mother
and how I use to make her laugh.

I think about the games she played
and how they never end,
I think about that very night
and how it all began.

I think about the past
that led to this situation,
I think about the Lord
and how He's blessing me with patience.

I think about the prayers
that's constantly going up for me,
I think about my God
and how He's there for my family.

I think about Mother Holts
and the things that she would say,
I think about the times
when she would teach me how to pray.

I think about my daddy
and all that he's been through
I think about the tears in his eyes
and what I shouldn't do.

[Hook]
I'm trying to tell you everything that I be really thinking
I'm trying to keep my eyes on the prize without so much as blinking
I'm trying to show you why people say that I wear my heart on my sleeve
I'm trying to tell you a story that some people just can't believe

"I Think About"

23 March 2012

I think about my friends
and a thing called loyalty,
I think about the reasons
why people don't show it to me.

I think about my family
and a thing that we call love,
I think about how all good things
come from the God above.

I think about Lil Jashe'
and the word achieve,
I think about what he can do
just as long as he believes.

I think about Japera
and how Mo. Holts be praying,
I think about a dream where
she leaves from where she was staying.

I think about Triumph
and its whole community,
I think about the battles
we've won against the enemy.

I think about my dreams
and a thing called prophecy,
I think about the things the Lord
really be trying to show to me.

I think about Mother Holts

and the things she wouldn't say,

I think about the times

when she'd encourage me to pray.

I think about my daddy

and all that we've put him through,

I think about the tears in his eyes

and what I wouldn't do.

[Hook]

I'm trying to tell you everything that I be really thinking

I'm trying to keep my eyes on the prize without so much as blinking

I'm trying to show you why people say that I wear my heart on my sleeve

I'm trying to tell you a story that some people just can't believe

"I Think About"

23 March 2012

I think about certain people
and how they carried me,
I think about them dying
and how scary it could be.

I think about the answers to
the questions that I want to ask,
I think about this journey
and if I'm really up to the task.

I think about the decisions
that I've made in my past,
I think about bad news
and how it always travels fast.

I think about the lessons
that I've learned so far in life,
I think about how failures
made me sharper than any knife

I think about the reason
why I do the things I do,
I think about the story
nobody wants to believe is true.

I think about the problems
and how they seem to follow me,
I think about the pain I feel
and how it makes me grit my teeth.

I think about Mother Holts
and the things she's gonna say,
I think about the times
when me and her would go and pray.

I think about my daddy
and all he's going through,
I think about the tears in his eyes
and what I'm gonna do.

[Hook]
I'm trying to tell you everything that I be really thinking
I'm trying to keep my eyes on the prize without so much as blinking
I'm trying to show you why people say that I wear my heart on my sleeve
I'm trying to tell you a story that some people just can't believe

"Not Plain But Simple"

23 April 2012

Sometimes I try to think ahead
but I just can't seem to think straight,
Can't close my eyes with steady breathing
because I lack the concentration to meditate.

I'm in another frame of mind
that is beyond your comprehension,
I believe that's why it seems hard
for me to keep your attention.

Beneath the intentions of my purpose
are foundations of ancient reign,
Tears falling out of season
coming from clouds full of pain.

My poetry is my inner hustle
and with it I sell clouds in a rainless season,
So with every line that you read
you get a dime bag of rhyme and reason.

Come step into my world
and hear the rhyme of my poetry,
And pay attention to what you hear
my truth might just set you free.

But you can't understand my words
until you begin to learn my thoughts,
And come to the realization
that my spirit and soul can't be store bought.

You should already know that
and truthfully I've seen you before,
Because I've been where you've been
I've even been you and more.

I stay sitting on the steps
that led to my poetry and song,
My mind altered and strained
because of journeys too long

So before you really mess up
and cut the strings to my violin,
I advise you to think twice
or drink a cup of my shaolin.

I'm really not a musician
but this poem has been instrumental,
They say deep down I'm a teacher
so the message is not plain but simple.

"Memorial Weekend"

25 May 2012

I'm sitting in my cell thinking
while trying to watch TV,
Thinking about my people
and other places I'd rather be.

This is Memorial Weekend
A time for family and fun,
But instead I'm sitting in jail
for something I did with a gun.

I miss all the excitement
and the walks around the street,
I miss eating over grandma's
and trying to steal me a seat.

I miss seeing all kinds of people
that I haven't seen in a year,
But I'm not going to see them this time
or the time after is what I fear.

I miss seeing old friends
that I haven't seen in awhile,
I miss all the "hey's" and "what's ups"
and the way that some would smile.

I miss seeing all the cars
and people crowded in the park,
I miss the cooking they do at the club
and the crows it brings after dark.

I miss waking up the next morning
thinking about the night before,
And knowing that at any moment
more family could walk through the door.

Once again I miss the excitement
and all the anticipation,
I miss sitting with my elders
and hearing their old conversation.

I really miss Sunday mornings
and the dinner we have that eve,
Most of all the banana pudding
Aunt Hazel makes before she leaves.

I miss all of the food
and the days we have fish fry's',
But I hate when the weekend ends
and people start saying all their good-byes.

Chapter 2

REFLECTIONS

OF MY

HEART

"My Final Plea"

8 August 2003

I really do miss you
and I have been for a while,
I miss our little talks
your pretty eyes and pretty smile.

I remember our first time
our first time being lovers,
We did it by the canal
with no bed or any covers.

Your parents would always try
what they could to keep us apart,
But we were brought together
by the powers in our heart.

Others really hated
hated to see us together,
Either walking down the street
or keeping warm in cold weather.

We always seemed to argue
even on the prettiest day,
Not over nothing serious
just because someone couldn't get their way.

We'd chill all day at the park
you and I would go back at night,
After about fifteen or twenty
we'd both walk away feeling right.

I know that we had problems
but now they all in the past,
We didn't run but we faced them
and yet our love still lasts.

I really do love you
and I know you have your doubt,
You doubt me I'll show you
that's really all I'm about.

In any voice you can tell I'm serious
despite of what others may say,
Because what matters is how we feel
and we both do feel the same way.

I know you'll be on my team
regardless of what I do,
Now I really am a man
and I'm trying to be with you.

In the past I made a promise
and that promise I plan to keep,
Whoever stands in my way
might end up falling asleep.

And if I am correct
the same promise you did make,
If you was hungry which would you choose
A piece of pie or a piece of cake.

"Talking To Myself"

14 December 2003

Frustration, aggravation
lack of understanding and pain,
These things that I've listed
I feel them everyday.

You know how I feel about you
you said that you felt the same,
But can't be with me 'cause you've been hurt
even though I'm not to blame.

I love your beautiful smile
and I always say that you're pretty,
You smile and then say thank you
but still you don't believe me.

What is it that I can do
to make you understand,
That this man really does love you
and really wants to be your man.

You said you can't take me seriously
but I've never lead you wrong,
Your head is full of doubts
but I'm the one keeping it strong.

You say you don't understand me
well I really don't understand you,
About us you still feel unsure
when I'm the one telling the truth.

81

I know I said before
all this will take time,
But time won't count for anything
when you always think that I'm lying.

Your heart is with someone else
I think you've said that before,
The longer that person keeps your heart
the faster I'm pushed out the door.

You say you try to talk to me
and you say I be acting weird,
But I'm the one who's listening
and your thoughts are all I hear.

I want to say forget it
throw in the towel and just quit,
I feel that if I continue
I'll be the one stuck in a pit.

In my mind I tell myself
I really do deserve better,
But in my heart I really feel
it's your storm I'd rather weather.

Call me dumb, call me weak
and say whatever you say,
I know I really want to be with her
and maybe ever marry her someday.

"Still Searching"

8 December 2003

I dream, I hope
I wish and I pray,
That I'll find someone
to love me one day.

I hurt, I stress
I cry and I grieve,
Is there really someone out there
someone out there for me.

I feel, I know
and I see what I need,
I told her before
but she didn't take heed.

It hurts to know that
someone you want you can't have,
It's like being real dirty
and not being able to take a bath.

Knowing the situation
my feelings haven't changed,
It really is the truth
even though it does sound strange.

I don't want another
and to be with her I do,
I'll give her whatever she wants
because my feelings are really true.

Her voice, her smile
and the way that she moves,
Regardless of all the mishaps
it's still her that I choose.

She knows what she wants
and she knows what she needs,
It's right here under her nose
but still she doesn't see.

She has a lot of dreams
and a lot of high hopes,
Which can easily be met
with the help of me, G. Holts.

I've said it in the past
and I'll say it again today,
If you doubt me then I'll show you
don't believe me then go and pray.

I know that I'm not perfect
but I am a part of the light,
Whether she sees it or not
I really am Mr. Right.

Too bad she can't love me
the way that she's suppose to,
Will I ever find someone
really I haven't a clue.

"Reasons For Everything"

9 December 2003

Why would I die for her
when she wouldn't die for me,
Maybe it's a feeling called love
which no one else can see.

Why would you do for her
when shc wouldn't do for you,
Like the color I represent
to her I'll always stay true.

Why do you continue
to listen to what she'd say,
Maybe it's because I believe
that we'll be together someday.

Why do you trust her
when she doesn't trust you at all,
Maybe that will change
when I catch her before she falls.

Why do you say you need her
when you're not the one she needs,
Maybe because without her
my heart will continue to bleed.

Why do you still love her
because against your heart she's committed treason,
I love her because I love her
and that's the very best reason.

Why do you love someone
who doesn't love you back,
It's because my mirrors still clear
and has not yet begun to crack.

How can you hold someone
that doesn't want to be held,
In my mind I pull these thoughts
but in my heart is where they dwell.

I may not be all human
but human for sure is my heart,
I just hope she sees the light
before it really gets too dark.

I cannot say a word
because I can't alter her decision,
But truthfully before it's too late
I hope on this He gives me permission.

I am really tired
of all my cries and all this pain,
But I know that without this girl
my life wouldn't be the same.

"How It Feels"

12 July 2006

Do you know how it feels

to want something really bad,

Even if you know nothing about it

or if it's something you never had.

Do you know how it feels

to look at something every day,

Always wanting to touch her

in every place and in every way.

Do you really know how it feels

to always have to bite your tongue,

Afraid of a negative response

or the fact that I'm just young.

Do you know how it feels

to start saying something then just quit,

Because you realize you can't tell this woman

how bad you want to hit.

Do you really know how it feels

to approach this woman you see,

Really not knowing at all

if she's even interested in me.

Do you really how it feels

to write a poem that she may read,

And to know that she will know

that these feelings do come from me.

"The Truth About Her"

12 February 2006

Ever since I first met her
she always seem to surprise,
Surprise me with her smile
and her very beautiful eyes.

I often catch myself
in my head saying her name,
And wondering if her feelings for me
could ever be the same.

At times I blame myself
for not asking that simple question,
And because I feared the response
I may have missed her true expression.

Many females try to gain
what she's had from the very start,
Something I watch very carefully
that special place that's called my heart.

Dang I wish she was here
just to see her pretty face,
And just to hear her beautiful voice
with her I would conversate.

Every man wants a good woman
from a teenager until he is grown,
But what I wish and truly want
is for her to be my own.

I've had many people tell me
keep waiting and I'll receive,
But the only thing I really want
is for her to be with me.

Whenever I close my eyes
and at night when I go to sleep,
I see myself with her
and I wish that we could be.

Could be together forever
have kids and then grow old,
But I believe that may be a story
that might never ever be told.

"I Hoped"

14 February 2006

I hoped I'd find someone
to help me with all this pain,
But I didn't expect to find someone
who'd take it all away.

I hoped I'd find someone
to make my life worthwhile,
But I didn't expect to find someone
who'd do that plus make me smile.

I hoped I'd find someone
who would spend most of their time with me,
But I didn't expect to find someone
until that time you made me see.

I hoped I'd find someone
to share my hopes and dreams,
But I didn't expect to find someone
to understand what it all really means.

I hoped I'd find someone
to my heart that wouldn't say nope,
But I didn't expect to find someone
who'd do that and give me hope.

I hoped I'd find someone
who was good at telling the truth,
But I didn't expect to find someone
even when I laid eyes on you.

I hoped I'd find someone
to be with on this special day,
But I didn't expect to find someone
who'd want more instead of the same.

I hoped I'd find someone
to be my valentine,
But I didn't expect to find someone
who also wanted to be mine.

"Someone Special"

15 April 2006

Have you ever met someone
who's caught you by surprise,
Someone with a beautiful smile
and very beautiful eyes.

Have you ever met someone
who could stop you in your tracks,
Someone you're willing to take risks for
without ever looking back.

Have you ever met someone
you always want to be around,
Someone you want to be with
but you're scared you'll get turned down.

Have you ever met someone
who you could spend your whole life wit',
But in her head the thought is possible
that to her you might not be it.

I've met that special someone
and I think of her everyday,
She really is something special
and I hope her feelings are the same.

"First Time"

1 February 2007

For the very first time
I seen her today,
And man when I looked at her
I didn't know what to say.

She was everything I expected
and maybe a little more,
I stared at her so much
I ended up making my eyes sore.

Beautiful from head to toe
Man! I love her eyes,
Really that's something I'd marry
and probably for her I would try.

Man this girl is cold
and really I'm just being real,
This girl is so damn fine
and got a body that really could kill.

But see there's a little problem
and it's something I really did see,
If I'm not tripping or mistaken
I don't think she was diggin' me.

She acted really shy
and very seldom looked my way,
Even when I tried to talk to her
she didn't have nothing to say.

"We May Be"

20 February 2007

A pretty blue color
unique in their own way,
They come with a face
I'd love to see everyday.

I look forward to seeing her
as if she looks forward to seeing me,
That I really don't know
but a fact it may just be.

Pretty hair and a pretty face
pretty eyes and a pretty smile,
Even being there in her presence
saying nothing would be worthwhile.

I'm telling you she's cold
and her body is just fine,
But the things I'm really after
it all lies in her mind.

Tell me something special
something I could possibly see,
Like me and her together
In the future we may be.

"A Special Comparison"

14 March 2007

Do you see how Pooh is sitting
and that smile that's on his face,
It's almost like he's not there
his mind is dwelling in another place.

That's exactly how I get
when I'm alone thinking about you,
My feelings for you are real
and I really am telling the truth.

I know your past was rough
and mine was rough as well,
It doesn't keep me from loving you
and this I know you can tell.

Regardless of what you hear
know that I'm all for you,
My feelings for you are strong
and I know that yours are too.

Poems are one of my ways
to express just how I feel,
So try to understand me
because baby this stuff is for real.

My love for you is strong
and that I want you to know,
Regardless of what goes down
for you my love will show.

I love you baby girl
this is something I really mean,
Never ever forget that
no matter how bad things may seem.

If you don't really understand
just listen to me when I speak,
The thorns represent hardships
and the stem represents me.

The leafs represents your friends
and the rose it represents you,
The top three leafs are flat and smaller
and I know that they are few.

The few that really love you
and never want to see you down,
But the leafs that are at the bottom
are the haters that love to clown.

Regardless of what's on the stem
it's you that's held up high,
And like this stem is doing
I'll be your support until you die.

You may have heard it before
but now it's coming from me,
If you doubt anything I tell you
in due time the truth you'll see.

"Lose His Head"

16 November 2007

One day he made a decision
and believe that it was smart,
Because without her his life was a mess
I mean his life was falling apart.

He loves her very much
she really was his homie,
Now that the temp has changed
she might not even know me.

He wrote this girl a letter
and hoped that it would change,
Didn't know what to expect
trying to get rid of all the pain.

He was hoping for a better life
something that she could provide,
He was wishing for her heart
because his feelings he could not hide.

Even though it would be better
he didn't know if she'd believe,
That God may have put them together
meaning she's suppose to be with me.

I often ask what we were waiting for
because others say just do it,
But really he was unsure
he doesn't know if he blew it.

Like the salmon in the river
who swims the other way,
With that determination I'll be waiting
for her each and every day.

The man who sleeps on the floor
can't really fall out of bed,
And a man who has no heart
can he really lose his head.

"Rejection"

20 November 2007

When I wake up in the morning
your face is all I see,
Wondering to myself
your reason for not wanting me.

I know you've been hurt before
but in that I played no part,
I'm just an ordinary person
trying to mend your broken heart.

I too have been hurt before
and this is very true,
But pain seems to be a feeling
that we all really must go through.

Without experiencing pain
we wouldn't know how it feels,
We wouldn't know how to smile
and we wouldn't know what was real.

Your past is what it is
I learned that a long time ago,
And if you let it dictate your future
you'll travel a dark lonely road.

"I Wrote About"

I grabbed my pen and paper
and then I began to write,
About how I really felt
and the things about you I liked.

I wrote about your smile
and how it makes me feel,
I wrote about a time
when your heart I was trying to steal.

When I met you I didn't have one
and you probably think that I'm lying,
But I only tried to steal yours
because you had already stolen mine

It may sound a little strange
but I'm only telling the truth,
Since the first time we ever met
I wanted to spend my life with you.

I wrote about your body
and the things we kept secret,'
Just in case I need to remember
my journal will always keep it.

I wrote a lot about
when around me the things you did,
You really acted so different
like the bad part you always hid.

Meaning you carried yourself
just like a perfect lady,
Instead of arguing and fighting
you'd kiss me and call me baby.

I wrote about how I think
you are the female of my dreams,
For me just perfect in every way
without nagging or hateful screams.

I wrote about how at first you thought
I was just a man of the street with no brain,
But after I showed you how smart I was
about me that thought did change.

I wrote about when I noticed
that your heart was opening up to me,
Go ahead and say what you will
but that was something I could clearly see.

Then I wrote about how your mind
and heart would play tug of war,
Because regardless of whoever you were with
to me you came back for more.

The last thing I wrote about
was the day you made me frown,
And as I was writing I got upset
so I decided to put the pen down.

"If I Need Someone"

22 January 2008

If I needed someone to talk to
could I count on you to listen,
For someone to hear my thoughts
for a while I have been wishing.

If I needed someone to help me
could you lend a helping hand,
The things that I'd say to you
would you try to understand

If I needed someone to hold me
would you open your arms and say,
No matter what I'm here to help you
and if I can't then together we'll pray.

If I needed someone to make me smile
could you put one on my face,
And if I needed to make that move
would take me to that place.

If I needed someone to go with me
would you be there by my side,
And regardless how bad things get
would stay or just go and hide.

"Reaching Out"

9 February 2008

First and foremost
I'd like to say congratulations,
For your new baby boy
for a while you've been waiting.

It's been a long time
since I've seen or heard from you,
I think about you all the time
and still love you, it's true.

I love you baby girl
this is something I really mean,
Never ever forget that
no matter how bad things may seem.

I was thinking the other day
and I reminded myself again,
It never fails for me in life
to always lose a friend.

I'm not trying to get you back
even though I wouldn't mind,
I'm just trying to get back the friendship
that we seemed to have left behind.

Every day it never fails
About you I seem to think,
I be wondering what you're doing
Especially when I start to drink.

103

I hope everything is well
and your baby is doing fine,
And every day Rev. Glover's voice
plays over and over in my mind.

I wanted to write this letter
to let you know that I wasn't mad,
I was told that you hated me
and that did make me sad.

I remember telling you before
and I'll tell you once again,
Regardless of whatever happens
you'll always be my friend.

Really it doesn't bother me
that your heart is with another man,
But not having you as a friend
hurts more than you understand.

Please don't think I'm crazy
obsessed or even insane,
It's just since I lost contact with you
I've been feeling a lot of pain.

I really don't blame you
but I only blame myself,
I really wanted to be with you
I didn't want anybody else.

If this letter seems to upset you
I really do apologize,
My heart made me write it
your still number one in my eyes.

I'll always be here for you
no matter what path you take in life,
And when your world starts getting dark
I will be your guiding light.

I hope you understand what I'm trying to say
and on your engagement for you I'm glad,
Just know your that special someone
that I always wish I had.

You don't have to respond to this letter
but if you ever had time,
Please just give me a call
Seven three three five five eight nine.

"Time For Me To Let Go"

12 February 2008

She said that she was cool
but I knew she was lying,
I had a feeling that it wouldn't last
But still I just kept trying.

I talked to her all the time
hoping that she was listening,
But I failed to see back then
that it was him that she was missing.

I tried real hard to make it work
but I was only wasting my time,
I should've known that I couldn't keep
something that was never mine.

Even though our journey was already over
I still kept holding on,
Thinking one day that she would come back
not knowing that I was wrong.

The way that girl made me feel
so many times I tried to explain,
But in the middle of my explanation
again I'm reminded of all the pain.

At times I try to keep a smile
on my face but it's hard to do,
I could say that I never seen it coming
but really it wasn't the truth.

Even though our time together was short
but to me it lasted awhile,
It's weird how someone who caused so much pain
when thought about could still make me smile.

I wrote a poem called Reaching Out
with intentions for her to see,
That regardless of what decision she made
she could always come back to me.

To make a long story short the poem was real
and her answer seemed to be so,
That's when I made the hardest decision
That it was time for me to let go.

"I Wont Let Go"

12 February 2008

I've been trying to let go
but it's been so hard to do,
No matter what I seem to be doing
I seem to always think about you.

Sometimes I listen to J. Holiday
whenever I'm playing the game,
It brings back a lot of memories
but without you it isn't the same.

I still remember that time
that we were laying in bed,
You were telling me about that person
and how he liked to mess with your head.

I gave you some advice
and for a while you seemed to take,
That's why I didn't understand it
when you repeated the same mistake.

Some people you can never change
regardless of how hard you try,
No matter how much you said you loved him
you came to me when he made you cry.

I'm suppose to let you go
but my heart can't handle that,
So I'll be waiting on the day
when you decide to come back.

"I Miss Because I Remember"

1 March 2008

Now that I think about it
it has been awhile,
Since I've written you a poem
just to make you smile.

I know I'm nowhere near you
so you can't hear what I say,
And even though I haven't seen you
in my head I see your face.

I miss the way you listened
every time I would try to share,
My wisdom and life experiences
and the way you played in my hair.

I miss the times you'd tell me
how you felt safe when I was around,
And anytime you could get away
we were meeting somewhere in town,.

I miss the way you'd smile
whenever I walked in the room,
Off your feet I was trying to sweep you
but you ended up holding the broom.

I miss the times you'd call me
when it was hard for you to go to sleep,
And no matter how late in the night it was
you would drive to be with me.

I miss trying to relax you
breathing deep your eyes would close,
And when it was time for them to open
it was me who loved you the most.

I miss how hard we'd laugh
while hiding at a certain spot,
And my shirt you were so quick to take off
when I claimed to be getting hot.

I miss the rides we use to take
at certain times to different cities,
I know what you wanted before you'd ask
because to yourself you'd say "that's pretty".

I miss the way you say the word cute
whenever I bought you a pair of shoes,
And while I'm driving you'd want to cuddle
asking me to put the car on cruise.

I miss the way you'd calm me down
when my emotions began to yell,
With your hand on my head you'd put your face in my neck
and man I really miss that smell.

I remember so many things
that's why it's you so much I miss,
I even remember the very first time
that from each other we had our first kiss.

"Getting Serious"

10 May 2011

You said that you like me
and yes I like you too,
Now the question seems to be
what are we going to do.

It doesn't matter to me
just as long as you're serious,
Because I myself have too
been a little serious.

Truthfully you have everything
to me that's how it seems,
I think about you everyday
I even see you in my dreams.

Since way back when we were kids I've
always had a crush on you,
But honestly I never thought
that the crush would really come true.

Now that we are older
I'd like to hold your hand,
Look into your eyes
and ask to be your man.

At first I was a little nervous
but now I'm back on track,
I'll do almost anything for you
and I'll always have your back

I'm determined to make you mine
that's what I plan to do,
My feelings are very strong
and those feeling are pointing at you.

I'm about to have a son
but don't let that turn you away,
I want you to be by my side
every minute, every hour, every day.

I hope in the back of your head
you're not having too many doubts,
If so just give me a chance
to show you what I'm all about.

Now I'm about to end this poem
but there's something I want to know,
Girl please can I be your man
and if I can then tell me so.

"My Heart Speaks"

19 August 2011

Wishing—hoping
Thinking—about you,
Wondering—smiling
About things—we use to do.

Your smile—I remember
How good—it made me feel,
The love—that we had
For each other—it was real.

Trying—to recall
The good times—that we had,
Trying—to understand it
When you left—I was sad.

Was it fear—was it worry
Or maybe—was it doubt,
Was it me—was it you
What it was—can't figure out.

Missing—you
The way—that I do,
I wonder—if that feeling
Is the same—within you.

Honestly—I don't know
If we—were meant to be,
But honestly—I do know
That it's you—I really see.

Hopefully—In the future
Maybe—we can be,
Together—me and you
A painted picture—I can see.

Maybe—in your heart
The spot for me—has been filled,
The cup of love—you once held
Full of mine—has been spilled.

Still—to the words
That he spoke—I'm holding on,
About me—about you
Being together—not alone.

Again—will I ever
Get to see you—time will tell,
In my heart—always
And forever—is where you dwell.

"Somewhere In Your Plans"

7 September 2011

I know you been watching me
and listening to what I say,
I feel you're a little disappointed
by the actions I commit every day.

Here lately I've been dealing
well you already know what's up,
With so much out here to drink
I'm still holding an empty cup.

You already know my thoughts
and you see what's in my heart,
Can you please give me an answer
or the real reason she wanted to part.

It really hurts me Father
to think that she didn't want me,
I gave a hundred and ten
but pain still seemed to haunt me.

I tried everything I could
to keep her mind on me,
But trusting for her was a problem
and that was something I came to see.

I'm tired of giving my love
but we both know that is a lie,
But I really didn't want to lose her
even though I just said goodbye.

I believe that I can wait
if we are really meant to be,
So if she is really mine
then can you please bring her back to me.

I'm sorry for all this babbling
but I'm feeling a whole lot of pain,
All together two years of sunshine
and twenty eight are full of rain.

Father I know I'm your child
so I'll leave it in your hands,
But still I ask concerning my life
include her somewhere in your plans.

"The Reason"

9 September 2011

I really couldn't see it
the reason why she left,
At first I couldn't believe it
it almost took my breath.

Its been about four long years
since I've seen or touched her hand,
And since the day that she left
I haven't been the same man.

Since two weeks and five days ago
she's been heavily on my mind,
And no matter how hard I try
I can't leave those thoughts behind.

I hope that she's okay
and nothing bad has crossed her path,
Honestly I really do miss her
and I love to hear her laugh.

I miss the way she'd smile
while looking me in my eyes,
Then say she knows what I'm thinking
and be right to my surprise.

I miss the way I felt
when we'd walk side by side,
And I'd love to hold her had
during the times we'd take a ride.

Even though I'm facing time
I still think in the back of my head,
That one day we're going to be together
and the opposite I really do dread.

I remember reading a story
about a man who wrote in a book,
And whatever it was he would write
in real life a place it took.

I thought about my journals
and that story I tried to copy it,
But of course to no surprise
it ended up being the opposite.

I guess I'll just keep hoping
just in case I won't hold my breath,
But still I can't understand it
the reason why she left.

"What Happened To You"

16 March 2004

Just like the sun rises
so can your fame,
And like it also falls
so can you and that's a shame.

Listen to me y'all
I'm not just talking stuff,
I aint trying to get on your nerves
And I really aint trying to fuss.

I'm an ordinary brother
trying to spit the truth,
And hopefully this message
will grab a hold of you.

Let's get it right y'all
I only want you to hear me,
I'm not trying to intimidate
or get you to fear me.

As I speak these words
and talk about fame,
Take heed to what I say
because only you will be to blame.

When a person gets famous
they also get a big head,
They attract fake friends
which are the haters that we dread.

But that's not all dawg
hell naw I'm not finished,
What used to be flawless
now has a big blemish.

What happened to you playa
you used to be real cool,
That fame went to your head
and that money started controlling you.

Your chilling with friends stopped
you really cut that short,
Then it seemed you got too good
to even sit with us on the porch.

Wow my dude
you played us real good,
You ruined our friendships
and disgraced your own hood.

Your brothers still loved you
even after you changed,
And since you got that money man
your mind aint been the same.

"I Still Don't Understand Why"

16 March 2007

Hey momma how you doing
I hope everything's okay,
It's been awhile since we've talked
and I'm missing you every day.

I've been going through a lot of problems
and dealing with a lot of pain,
Since that day I left your house
my life hasn't been the same.

I dream about the past
and the things you've done to me,
I know you asked for forgiveness
but there's a lot that you can't see.

For seventeen years of my life
you kept me in a state of fear,
Abuse both verbal and physical
my cries no one seemed to hear.

Daddy was the only person
that I considered to be a friend,
No matter what he had my back
and protected me until the end.

I honestly don't know what I done
to make you treat me the way you did,
If it was because I looked like my father
I couldn't help that I was his.

122

"Like A Mother"

20 May 2008

Even though you're not my mother
I still have a lot to say,
You've had my back since we were kids
every month, every week, every day.

You've always been there for me
even when there wasn't a need,
Even though I was born your cousin
you'll always be my sister to me.

You always tried to support me
in whatever I tried to do,
I only thought I had Mo. Holts
but I know now that I have you.

Regardless of what it is
I'll always have your back
And regardless of what I do
I know you'll keep me on track

For the son I'm about to have
there's some things I need to attain,
So I'm going to need you even more
especially through all of the pain.

This poem is a little thank you
for helping me on my way,
So I thank you, Angel very much
and Happy Mothers Day.

"Take Heed"

21 June 2008

There's something I'll admit
things did get out of control,
But in the midst of all this drama
was something I didn't know.

For what reason it may be
I really don't have a clue,
But I feel that something aint right
that's why I'm writing you.

I knew about old girl
And your name you knew I wouldn't spit,
Until your cousin Michael
said her flame you may have lit.

Meaning that you got her pregnant
you busted in baby girl,
And you know as well as I do
if true would crush Angel's world.

After a certain point in time
our agreement was simple and plain,
But getting another girl pregnant
man that mess is insane.

You know that girl's my sister
and I love that girl to death,
Besides the kids she's the only person
I'd give my last and final breath.

She's always been there to help me
even when no help was needed,
I told you to do what you do
don't break her heart was all I pleaded.

Really what I'm trying to say
is this time you crossed the line,
That's why I said what I said to Angel
I didn't know that Michael was lyin'.

On the real I never mention
that she might be having your child,
Because I didn't know if it was true
and plus that mess would have drove Angel wild

But truthfully I really was wondering
why your cousin was starting to flip,
But before I really could talk to you
in a text you started running your lip.

I know I ran mine too
but really I couldn't believe,
In that text you threatened my life
which was something I couldn't conceive.

Man you threatened my life
and I took that threat to heart,
Regardless of the problems we had
that type of threat I would never start.

That shit really bothered me bad
and my mind it sort of went blank,
At the time I read that text
your ass I vowed to spank.

Damn I wish you would have never
ever had made that statement,
On a list with all my enemies
your name I was ready to place it.

In that field you have no experience
compared to me you're just a kid,
I'm not talking about your age
but the thought you had in your lid.

The reason I haven't touched you
is because I remember the promise I made,
But know that I really was ready
for that text to make you pay.

But I began to think about Triumph
and through it the things I've learned
I know Satan is always working
and friendships he tries to burn.

So Jamal I do forgive you
and hope in you this poem plants a seed,
Try to remember the point I made
and to that point please take heed.

"You Tore My Life Apart"

21 April 2011

At first I will admit
with you I was very angry,
I wanted to hurt you bad
because of how you betrayed me.

I really don't understand it
because you said I was your friend,
You was the one that even suggested
to bring my fear to a certain end.

I was moved by your proposal
and I really could not believe,
That somebody actually wanted to help
remove a fear but do it for me.

We've known each other since high school
and for you I would risk my life,
Because you was one of the few
that kept it real and treated me right.

You always had my back
regardless of what we did,
It was like I have always known you
like you knew me since I was a kid.

But really I cannot blame you
because actually what I did was worse,
I killed one of my childhood friends
who I've known almost since birth.

130

I looked at you like a brother
even though I had one of my own,
Anytime you went on a mission
you never had to do it alone.

I remember when you went to prison
no one else could have treated you better,
All the time I couldn't send money
but you always received a letter.

I remember when you would write
about a friend who was always true,
When I wrote back asking who it was
you replied "my nigga it's you".

So man I can actually say
I forgive you with all my heart,
But know you really did hurt me
and that you tore my life apart.

"My Letter To God"

Dear God,
I was told to write you a letter
but I really don't know what to say,
Because you already know my heart
and what I've done each and every day.

Well as you already know
I've been through a lot of pain,
I've done a lot of wrong
but in my life you still sustain.

Sometimes I'd wonder why
bad things seem to happen to me,
Some things I brought on myself
but others, reasons I really can't see.

Like what did I do to my mother
to make her treat me the way she did,
Was I that much of a nuisance
or ever worse that bad of a kid.

How come she use to call me crazy
and all kinds of hurtful names,
It was like she was making a sacrifice
and we were the ones being slain.

I know I said I forgive her
but why can't I let it all go,
It's like no matter how hard I try
through me the pain always seems to flow.

132

What did I do to Nikki

to make he do what she did with David,

I remember when she'd try to explain

but because I was hurting I told her to save it.

How come Yolanda made that decision

like we wasn't ever trying to be together,

It was like I was her umbrella

but she threw me away along with the weather.

Now I know that she had some issues

but why did Ke' trip the way she did,

I didn't even do anything to her

I even helped take care of her kid.

How come Erika just upped and left

even after we had that conversation,

Did she not understand Reverend Glover

when he said that we needed to have patience.

Why'd Ashley trip the way she did

before she even had my son,

She acted like I was all hers

before a relationship had even begun.

How come she didn't even tell me

that she was about to go into labor,

She didn't even give him my last name

I didn't get a chance to even sign the paper.

Can you tell me why Crystal left me

even after she promised she'd stay,

Was it because of another man

or the price of her heart I couldn't afford to pay.

God what did I do to Tony
to make him betray our trust,
I know I shouldn't question your plans
but for some reason I feel like I must.

Why does it seem so hard for people to love me
and why am I always surrounded by drama,
It's been going on since I can remember
thinking back it started with momma.

How come when I played for the Raiders
some of the players they treated me bad,
They would call me these hateful names
made racist jokes which made me sad.

Besides you, how come when I talk
nobody really seems to listen,
I either have to write them a poem
or express that it's them that I'm missin'.

How come I feel like everybody owes me
A little bit of their time,
And when I don't really seem to get it
I feel neglected and end up cryin'.

For me to be a good person
why do I change so much when I get mad,
I even make those who are around me
feel empty or feel really sad.

What kind of spirit was in me
to cause me to take their life,
Was it him or something within me
that made me do what I did that night.

God do I really have a problem
or is the devil just stomping my toe,
Really I don't know the answer
so could you please just let me know.

I know I have to stay strong
but why is it so hard to do,
Sometimes I think I am nothing
and sometimes I believe it is true.

I know I'm in jail for murder
but is it for something that I failed to do,
Like being a sinner for all these years
and being hard headed not listening to you.

I know that it says in the scriptures
it's your will to save us all,
But when I change and try to stand for you
I always manage to fall.

To you I've made a lot of promises'
that I always seem to break
God I really am sorry
and my apology I hope you take.

God how could you love me so much
considering all the evil I've done,
It's been times to you I wouldn't listen
even at times I ignored your son.

I know everything happens for a reason
but still I just don't understand,
And I know we must have faith
because it's all a part of your plan.

It's sad that it comes to this
for you to really get my attention,
I just pray you're not fed up
and still see fit to give me redemption

Right now I'm trying my best
and I'm beginning to strengthen my faith,
Please God give me one more chance
don't let the world just take me away.

Why'd you allow Lil Rut to get shot
when he was just looking for a ride,
I still remember the day I found out
I couldn't do nothing but break down and cry.

Why couldn't I see Daddy Bill
before the day that he was to die,
I just wished you'd allowed me to see him
so I could have at least said goodbye.

How come Markelle died the way he did
in his sleep he didn't have a chance,
Why'd it take so long for them to get there
I mean the help was just at a glance.

How come I keep disappointing my father
when the opposite is all I've been trying,
It hurt me to look at his face
because when he seen me he couldn't stop crying.

Now I'm not trying to be disrespectful
by asking questions about what you allow,
I just really don't understand it
I mean really I don't understand how.

I want to thank you for all you've done
and keeping me alive since the time of my birth,
Even though I've been through a lot
I understand it could have been worse.

I thank you for Mother Holts
and the teaching she put in my father,
Because I know if it wasn't for him
to respect my mother I wouldn't even bother.

I thank you for all the people
you've allowed in and out of my life,
I even thank you for the ones that hurt me
and especially for the ones that did me right.

I thank you for my younger sister
even though at times she gets on my nerves,
Anytime she was ever in need
if I had it she knew it was hers.

I thank you for my younger brother
even though he use to make me mad,
But knowing that he use to look up to me
Made me feel special which is more than glad.

I thank you for my older sister Angel
even though you know she's really my cousin,
Anytime that I would mess something up
she was right there in my ear always fussin'.

I thank you for the trials you brought me through
the ups and downs, pain and heartaches,
Even though they may have been painful
without them I wouldn't have learned to appreciate.

I thank you for my Uncle Rick
Mother Newman and again Mother Holts too,
Because honestly if it wasn't for them
I wouldn't have learned to appreciate you.

I thank you for First Sergeant York
who helped me get out of the Army,
And I thank you for sending your son
for what he did it's harder for sin to harm me.

I thank you for all of my teachers
that wouldn't let me just breeze through school,
Because of them I am very smart
and can't no man ever call me a dumb fool.

I thank you for all of the parents
when away from home that kept me on track,
And I thank you for some of their children
who became friends and they had my back.

I thank you for the dreams that I have
even though I don't know what some mean,
I will admit that some do scare me
and others are not what they seem.

I thank you for me being in jail
even though it's something I dread,
Because if it wasn't for me being locked up
the scriptures wouldn't be in my head.

I thank you for me meeting Ashley
because through her you blessed me with a child,
Even though I really don't get to see him
when I think about him he still makes me smile.

I thank you for this gift of writing
I can do wonders with a pencil and pen,
Some of my poems have some people crying
and some make them smile for that I thank you again.

"Happy Father's Day"

15 June 2011

Even though I'm sitting in jail
you was still good at what you did,
Meaning that you didn't fail
when it came to raising this kid.

Daddy you was always there
and you really did do a great job,
Between you and Mother Holts
my life's been hard for the devil to rob.

I know I didn't turn out perfect
still you raised a very good man,
Until now I've never been to jail
and no woman has felt my hand.

You taught me a lot about respect
and it's stuck with me since the beginning,
Since I've been playing this game called life
you're one of the reasons that I've been winning.

Growing up in a house with Corrina
the environment was stressful and tight,
But no matter how much pain I endured
you were always there to make it right.

So I hope you're thinking clearly
and understand what I'm trying to say,
I thank you for always being there
I love you and Happy Fathers Day.

"Dear Reverend Glover"

25 August 2011

I know this looks like a poem
but really it's a letter,
Whenever I write this way
my thoughts they come out better.

If I am not mistaken
I believe it's been four years,
Since the last time that I saw you
in your church with eyes full of tears.

I don't know if you can remember r
but there was a girl that came with me,
We've been friends for about two years
and what came next I really didn't see.

The next day after we left your church
she was no longer by my side,
She said that she wouldn't leave me
but that day I found out she lied.

From then on something in me changed
and really I know that it shouldn't,
I tried to take heed to your words
but back then I was weak so I couldn't.

Two years later I went to California
then the Lord blessed me to come back,
Still then I just wouldn't listen
and continued to stay on the wrong track.

142

In May of 2010
I went to Lexington to look for employment,
Six months later I found a good job
and it brought me a lot of enjoyment.

The Lord blessed me with a good job
then He blessed me with a place of my own,
Even though I was doing pretty good
I still felt as if I were alone.

One day when I was at work
in my mind I went someplace else,
I started thinking about my future
and what I had I didn't get myself.

Then I thought about your message
and I could almost hear your voice,
Right then it was like something hit me
and I knew that I had to make a choice.

Scriptures say you have to confess
and ask the Lord to forgive your sins,
I then thought about my past
but was scared to turn myself in.

I knew I would have to tell
about what I did back in 2005,
I knew that I couldn't get right with the Lord
while I was holding onto that lie.

Well I have known all my life
that God works in mysterious ways,
But I really had no idea
He'd start a mystery in the following days.

The evening of March the 27th
I was visited by an old friend,
I talked to him about my past
not knowing my freedom would end.

Two days later I was arrested
and there was something I couldn't believe,
After telling the police what I did
I felt free and truly relieved.

After spending a month in jail
I began to read the word,
It was like it was the first time I read it
because the words I actually heard.

It's been about five months
since I've been locked up in jail,
Gods changed the way I think
I don't curse or worry about hell.

Every now and then when I'm reading
in my head I hear your voice,
I smile and then thank God
for allowing me to make that choice.

Allowing me to choose to serve him
regardless of my situation,
And that message you sent through Mo. Holts
has encouraged me to have more patience.

God has touched my mind
and he has also touched my heart,
But all this mess I could have avoided
if I had made this choice from the start.

I am really able to understand
A lot of what I read,
And I'm sure this phrase is a fact
that God is all I need.

It took God to sit me down
and put me in a place,
To understand how important it was
and how much I need to have faith.

Faith assures us of things we except
and convinces us of the things we cannot see,
God accepts people because of their faith
and because of my faith I believe he accepts me.

Now there's questions that I'll need answered
and Mo. Holts she does her best,
But since you are closer to God
I figured you could answer the rest.

When I have a question she can't answer
you are the first to come to my mind,
So I'm asking if you would help
on my journey in leaving the world behind.

I'm studying the scriptures daily
I'm fasting and still praying,
I'm going to hold on to Gods word
no matter what people in here are saying.

Most of all I want to say thank you
and know that in me you watered a seed,
Four years ago you spoke with such authority
it was like you; how I wanted God to use me.

I want to be that close to God
and like you live on nothing but faith,
I hope to hear from you soon
and keep me in mind whenever you pray.

"Always Always"

8 September 2011

Since the very beginning
you've been here by my side,
You've helped to make me smile
at times when I should have cried.

At first I was really scared
but you helped take away that fear,
Because you always let me know
That you and God was always near.

I remember you had an idea
you told me to write God a Letter,
You said it would do me some good
and it made me feel a lot better.

You always came to see me
and you put money on the phone,
You always seemed to let me know
no matter what that I wasn't alone.

I'm glad that you were here
and when everything went down,
Because I needed a mother figure
and without one I'd be wearing a frown.

I'm really glad that you are here
to help me get through these days,
I thank you and know that I love you
No matter what always always.

"A Letter To Corrina"

12 December 2011

How are you doing momma
I hope everything is ok,
I was surprised to hear from you
through the card that I received today.

I have been doing alright
but I wish that I could go home,
I'm tired of being in jail
and at times tired of feeling alone.

I'm going to ask you a question
because the answer I just cant see,
Why didn't you talk to that lady
knowing that what you said could've helped me.

At that time I thought you would help
but you didn't and I don't know why,
When I was told that you refused to talk
I couldn't do nothing but sit here and cry.

In case you don't already know
they're trying to give me life in the pen,
That means I'll never get to be free
or see the outside world again.

Now nobody's trying to point any fingers
or try to put the blame on you,
They're just really trying to figure out
what set me off and they want the truth.

See these people they ran some tests
and they just can't figure it out,
Since they can't get it out of my present
they want to know what my past is about.

At first I was a little upset that
you wouldn't help me weather this storm,
Especially because you say that you love me
and better yet knowing that I'm you r first born.

But everything is going to be fine
as long as we all just believe,
We must all continue to have faith
even if the future we cannot see.

So tell me about your new place
and the reason you decided to move,
Did you find a good looking man
and you are trying to get back your groove.

Now that I think about it
I do remember that snowball fight,
I don't remember breaking that mirror
but have done it is something I might.

I remember this particular Christmas that
there were unwrapped presents under the tree,
And of course to my surprise
most of those presents did belong to me.

I remember the time we got bikes
I believe they were called Diamondbacks,
We would always run into the garage door
and I remember how much you didn't like that.

We did have some pretty good times
well the ones that I can remember,
That's the reason besides October
my favorite month happens to be December.

Well momma I'll let you go
and know that I love you too,
I know that you love me as well
because we're family and that's what we do.

Chapter 4

REFLECTIONS

OF  MY

LIFE

"My Big Mistake"

20 February 2004

I sit in my room
and just talk to myself,
And at the end of the conversation
I realize that I need help.

I start feeling kind of funny
and I get a little scared,
Then my scalp gets hot
I even feel the heat in my hair.

I don't get this feeling
but every now and then,
But before it gets to strong
I go and spend about ten.

I've had a lot of people tell me
most of the ones I let read,
That my poems are real good
because they're real and they're deep.

I don't use big fancy words
well sometimes I really do,
But only for lyrical reasons
not trying to confuse you.

My first time on my own
I lost track of my goals,
Didn't want to listen to nobody
just sell drugs and get blowed.

I know it wasn't right
but I was having too much fun,
Not thinking about my future
just living the fast life which was dumb.

I didn't see it at the time
but I knew it would come to an end,
Whether in the streets or not
I'd end up dead or in the pen.

But hustling wasn't my problem
it was something deeper than that,
The problem was in my head
because of some things from way back.

I know this poem is long
but I got to tell my story,
Just learn from my mistake
and let that knowledge be your glory.

I'm not trying to be bossy
or tell you what to do,
I'm just an ordinary brother
speaking nothing but the truth.

Like now you hear this poem
and your thought is probably "man",
So now that you're ready to listen
I'm gonna talk about Uncle Sam.

Not saying the Army's bad
but that stuff just wasn't for me,
That's why I didn't serve three years
I served one, four months and a week.

Now don't get a brother twisted
because I'm really not a punk,
I just paid for a mistake
that I made coming out the trunk.

I was very hard headed
because daddy told me to come home,
Not trying to make excuses
I didn't because I was hurt and feeling alone.

I bet you thinking now
what's this got to do with the Army,
Truthfully I wanted a new start
not thinking that it would harm me.

Now that was my big mistake
not listening to what daddy said,
Because instead of losing my problems
I gained more and lost my head.

But I truly thank God
for sending somebody to help me,
His name was First Sergeant York
A white man who felt me.

He seen that I had a problem
and tried to help me out,
Unlike everybody else around me
he didn't judge or block me out.

He said what he had to say
and did what he had to do,
Then one day he approached me
And said "I believe I just helped you".

I gave him a funny look
and asked what he was talking about,
He said I did what you asked
Private Holts you're getting out.

I really was happy
but I knew I'd never be the same,
Because of being hard headed
damn near drove me insane.

I didn't go all the way
but I was right there in the head,
And about one year later
Daddy Bill had been pronounced dead.

If you didn't feel this poem
then you didn't really feel me,
But hopefully you listened to the words
and got the moral of this story.

"My One and Only"

9 June 2008

Five pounds, seven ounces
and fifteen inches in height,
My second born came into this world
and yes I'm feeling right.

Eight years and seven months y'all
is really a very long time,
But the wait was really worth it
to finally get what was already mine.

When I first laid eyes on him
I put my hand over my mouth
I turned my head and closed my eyes
that's when the tears started rolling out.

That is my little boy
and I believe that he is the key,
My blood runs through his veins
God said he belongs to me.

He's the key to that lock
the big one on that door,
The door that'll hold my wrongs
to be locked away forever more.

I'm happy to have a son
now I have a new little homie,
Since my first is dead and gone
he's now my one and only.

"Your Reflection"

13 July 2009

[Hook] (Verse 1)
When I look in the mirror
all I see staring back is your reflection,
I bow my head and then thank God
because you are a blessing.

Every night before I close my eyes
I hit my knees and then I pray,
I pray that the love you have for me
no matter what in your heart it'll stay.

I remember like yesterday
November 24th 1996,
That's when I became a father
had me feeling like I was the shit.

I wanted to tell my momma
but I knew that I really couldn't,
I almost told my father
but something said I shouldn't.

So I did my best to keep
my secret quiet on the low,
Didn't tell nobody nothing
didn't even let my brother know.

To tell my family about him
so hard she'd get me to try,
She said it hurt and let me know
that it tore her up inside.

Two years and eleven months
if I'm not mistaken was the time,
That I chose to tell my family
and put a stop to one big lie.

But before I could even tell them
I heard the news and then I cried,
November 21st 1999
that's when they say my boy had died.

[Hook] (Verse 2)
When I look in the mirror
all I see staring back is you reflection,
I bow my head and then thank God
because you are a blessing.

Every night before I close my eyes
I hit my knees and then I pray,
I pray that the love you have for me
no matter what in your heart it'll stay.

Since then I always prayed
to send me another seed,
And almost nine years later
A son was born to me.

He was just so much like David
from what he did to the way he laughed,
Even though they were two different bodies
between both his spirit passed.

This time didn't keep any secrets
told everybody that I could,
I didn't want to tell my mother
but something said I should.

And the first time that I saw him
I couldn't do nothing but cry,
It took me a while to hold him
didn't ask because they knew why.

Three months after he came home
all those feelings went away,
I knew then I had my son
he just had another face.

The answer to my prayers
he truly is a blessing,
And every time that I look in the mirror
all I see is your reflection.

[Hook] (Verse 3)
When I look in the mirror
all I see staring back is your reflection,
I bow my head and then thank God
because you are a blessing.

Every night before I close my eyes
I hit my knees and then I pray,
I pray that the love you have for me
no matter what in your heart it'll stay.

We took him to Bowling Green
after some time had passed,
During the time he spent with my father
was the hardest I heard him laugh.

That's when my father told me
that he knew what was in my head,
Instead of giving a lecture
he played with Mal' instead.

As I sat and watched him play
with him on the kitchen table,
I knew deep down inside
my life would have to be stable.

In order for me to raise
A son like my father did,
In order for me to mold
A man over time from a kid.

I made my hardest decision
to leave my son behind,
I had to prepare his future
before I ran out of time.

Now that I'm on my journey
there is no time for resting,
And every time that I look in a mirror
all I see is your reflection.

[Hook] (2x)
When I look in the mirror
all I see staring back is your reflection,
I bow my head and then thank God
because you are a blessing.

Every night before I close my eyes
I hit my knees and then I pray,
I pray that the love you have for me
no matter what in your heart it'll stay.

"A Hug, Kiss, and A Choke"

25 December 2011

I was thinking about my father
and the things that we used to do,
I remember how we didn't like
for him to drive us to school.

It was because of the car he drove
that's why we always tried to hide,
Instead of letting us out in front of the school
we wanted to be let out on the side.

Whenever he came to the house
we knew it was time to play,
"Y'all can come spend the night with me"
was something we couldn't wait for him to say.

Don't get me wrong we loved our mother
but she kept us all full of fears,
But our father was always there
no matter what to wipe away the tears.

We were all in a different world
whenever we spent time with our father,
Our mother, our problems, our fears
when with him to us didn't bother.

163

I remember when we were kids
he used to play basketball games on the hill,
We'd love to go up there with him
to play with our friends or just sit there and chill.

We always wanted to be around daddy
for reasons that's not know,
We'd rather be bored with our father
than have fun with our friends back at home.

Sunday mornings he'd fix us all breakfast
biscuits, rice, sometimes grits, and eggs,
Then we'd sit down to watch the Cowboys
and watch Emmitt do wonders with his legs.

Another memory just came to my mind
it's one I don't like to admit,
Playing Mario when he lived in J-5
always losing so I had to pass the stick.

Our time with him was always enjoyable
whether bored, sick, or even broke,
And I miss how when we had to go to bed
he'd tuck us in with a hug, kiss, and a choke.

"He Thought They Were Only Names"

7 February 2012

Born in 1980
Gilbert Jr. came to be,
A spitting image of his father
A truth that others couldn't help but see.

As time gradually went on
Lil Gilbert became a little older,
And the older he seemed to get
the more girls began to use his shoulder.

Most of his friends seemed to be females
and in that he took a little pride,
Some came to him for protection
and others only came when they cried.

When with these females it was like a job
and he truly wasn't the same,
Because of that and an idea from a movie
he decided to adopt another name.

Soon he became Dequaun
though it was a name he barely used,
He'd only use it in certain places
and sometimes whenever he'd choose.

That name also came with a spirit
but at the time he just didn't see,
He just figured it was a part of his character
so that's who he was just going to be.

That spirit kept him intertwined with females
and it took a big toll on his heart,
It caused him to be a little colder
and most of all 'bout tore his mind apart.

Selling drugs and running the streets
and joining a gang caused him to see,
That within him was yet another person
and he gave him the name B.G.

Now B.G. was the worst of the three
and believe me this part was fearless,
No matter what, he did what he wanted
and when feeling pain this part remained tearless.

With him fighting the other two
all the time seemed to make him stronger,
And when this part would come to the surface
over time it started staying a little longer.

Whenever Gilbert was at his weakest
B.G. would use drugs to help him out,
He used liquor, weed, and pills
then gave him cocaine to put up his snout.

Now Dequaun brought the urge for females
which brought him pain, stress, and confusion,
But B.G. brought everything else
including hate and the drugs he was abusing.

Over time Lil Gilbert lost control
but thought he still had it which was sad,
He began to fall apart on the inside
and past problems almost drove him mad.

By not knowing what was really going on
he couldn't get a grasp on himself,
He didn't know about these other spirits
but he knew that he really needed help.

So God allowed him to be in a position
where he couldn't run and had to stay still,
Using his word, his son, and his love
He removed these spirits at will.

He had to believe that Christ
died to take away his sins,
And that he was Gods only begotten son
which is where our faith really begins.

Now it didn't happen all at once
but took place in a number of stages,
He then had to confess his sins
like the confession he wrote on these pages.

After that he began studying the word
trying to live in the creators light,
Reading the old and new testaments
trying to decipher the wrongs from right.

He began to pray more often
and with that he began to fast,
He wants to stay close to God
so the joy inside him will last.

It's almost been a year
And his position is still the same,
Even still it's hard to believe
Because he thought they were only names.

Chapter 5

REFLECTIONS

OF MY

FAITH

"What Mother Holts Said"

1 April 2004

There once was a boy
who had very big plans,
Dreams of making it big
and growing to be a good man.

This boy left the yard
and he was not yet ready,
Didn't know the streets was that rough
and turned out to be so petty.

Another brotha in the streets
something really not needed,
Don't smoke weed or hustle son
was all his father pleaded.

Stay away from evil
and try to get saved
These words from Mother Holts
stayed in his head every day.

God said it could be done
but didn't say that it would be easy,
That's why trying to live righteous
ain't all fun and games or even cheesy.

You've got to be serious
because you could lose your soul,
If your names not in the book
to Heaven you will not go.

Hell is really a place
where you don't want to be,
Let God lead your life
because unlike you He can see.

He can see all your ups
and He can see all your downs,
Any trouble that you're in
He can surely bring you out.

Just keep faith in God
and always try to have patience,
Because He will reward you
and that is not to be mistaken.

We'll talk later on
whenever you get the chance,
Just take time to listen
and really try to understand.

Don't forget to always pray
because to heaven you want to go,
I don't want to see you lost
and end up losing your soul.

"A Promise"

24 August 2006

As I got out of my seat
I started feeling heavy,
The true reason I know not
but I don't think I was ready.

I tried really hard
to keep myself together,
But unlike a strong foundation
I fell in this stormy weather.

Every step that I seemed to take
the pain it seemed to increase,
It all seemed so real
but yet I was still asleep.

The room started getting cold
well at least that's how it felt,
Now I'm wondering to myself
what cards have I been dealt.

If only I could wake up
and return to my normal self,
But waking up from a dream like this
I knew I would need some help.

I tried to call out names
but no sound was coming out,
What in the world is going on
how come I can't use my mouth.

Now I'm starting to get nervous
but mainly I'm really afraid,
Is this really just a dream
or for my sins is it time to pay.

I never seen this coming
I thought I was just asleep,
I even thought for a minute
that my mind was playing tricks on me.

Please don't let this be
be the time for me to cash in,
I promise I'll get it right
just give me a chance to do it again.

Then I heard a voice say
get up before you're late,
I opened my eyes and see
that I was looking in Mother Holts face.

I told her about my scary dream
and the price that I almost paid,
That's when she turned her head and said
just remember the promise you made.

"His Message"

9 march 2007

You're sitting here alone
wondering what to do,
You're feeling out of place
and you really don't have a clue.

All your reasons for pain
has now become excuses,
Blaming mainly your mother
because she was abusive.

A man is only a man
if he can stand on his own,
Regardless of what's up against him
and even if he is alone.

I sit and watch you at times
especially when you cry,
No matter how hard things may get
you should never wish to die.

Your life is something precious
it's your ticket into heaven,
This you have been taught
since before the age eleven.

Keep strong and stay faithful
and always believe in me,
My breath is in your body
therefore you are my seed.

Listen to your grandmother
because she only speaks the truth,
It's a message I've been sending
since way before your youth.

You should learn to listen
because it's something that you need,
Especially if you really plan
to spend eternity here with me.

"Our Shepherd"

14 May 2008

Way back in fifty-nine
to her God did reveal,
To reopen the doors of the church
and to this day she is here still.

Satan knew God had chosen her
because she'd obey Gods law and not mans,
She's been through trials and tribulations
but on her feet is where she stands.

Led by the power of God
and filled with the Holy Ghost,
God chose to keep her here
because it was where she was needed the most.

Full of wisdom, power, and faith
she puts us in them mind of Job,
Regardless of what's up against her
through her, God's goodness did show.

She stayed true through all her struggles
and even through all of her fears,
And the word and encouragement she got from God
was like music to her ears.

The more work she tried to do
the more Satan tried to take away,

178

He started with her and then her family
but God always kept them safe.

Being obedient to God's word
for her hasn't been a problem,
All the troubles that was thrown her way
God was always there to solve them.

The pastor of this church
she has been since fifty-nine,
Striving to move forward with
the thought of leaving no souls behind.

Here at Triumph the Church
And Kingdom of God in Christ,
The church of the first born
she has been our guiding light.

God has always provided for her
all the things that she needs,
And I know that inside a lot of people
she's sown a lot of seeds.

Now to me and everyone else
that shows a lot of dedication,
She's put up with a lot of people
and stayed full of determination.

Forty-nine years
is for real a very long time,
She's followed the instructions of God
without ever asking him why.

"Another Message"

3 April 2011

Stop trying to fix everything
because it's not for you to fix,
I can see you're tired of hardships
and falling for Satan's tricks.

Like now you're in a position
that you've never been in before,
You're wondering what's going to happen
and if you're going to win the war.

I've watched you all your life
and I know all that you have done,
I've seen the times you've stood and fought
and the times you chose to run.

Everything happens for a reason
even if you don't understand,
Just know that I have control
and it's all a part of my plan.

You hurt so much inside
and at times you don't know why,
When you can't fix something in life
you break down and begin to cry.

Now listen to what I tell you
because you can always trust in me,
Know that your sins have been forgiven
because in me you do believe.

I've always been there with you
even when you've felt alone,
I'm the one who gave you the speed
to run away from your mother's home.

Your mother is truly sorry
but she can't erase the pain,
She did ask for forgiveness
and I heard when you did the same.

Just give your life to me
and everything will be okay,
Even when times seem to be hard
don't get discouraged just get down and pray.

This trial you're going through now
believe it won't last forever,
Just remember I'm always with you
and leave you is something I'll never.

"Faith"

23 April 2011

I believe in God the Father Almighty
the maker of heaven and earth,
That's the beginning of the Triumph Creed
that's been recited since before my birth.

Even though I've never seen him
or even actually heard his voice,
But when he speaks through other people
I try to listen which is my choice.

Some may even ask how
you believe in something that you can't see,
Even though I cannot see him
I know he resides in you and me.

It may not be as strong as it should be
but believe me when I say that I have faith,
It's the reason I get on my knees
and close my eyes and then begin to pray.

Faith enabled Enoch
to be taken up instead of dying,
One day my faith will be that strong
and until it is I'll just keep trying.

Faith led Moses to leave Egypt
without being afraid of the kings anger,
Faith had people looking forward
for God's word who was born in a manger.

Faith led the prostitute Rahab
to welcome the spies as friends,
That faith in turn saved her family
while all others had to see their ends.

Faith caused Israel to cross the Red Sea
as if it were dry land,
Faith caused the walls of Jericho
to fall under God's mighty hand.

Faith leads me to believe
that my God is truly real,
And that He saves all who comes to him
from the devil who tries to kill.

Faith led Mother Newman to pray
even after her grandson's death,
That same faith through all of his trials
was the reason Jesus gave his last breath.

Faith directs our lives
even if you don't believe it,
God's grace through faith is really what saves us
so at all costs you must achieve it.

I hope that you have listened
to the words that's in this poem,
And if you don't really know Jesus
I advise that you get to know him.

"I Am Who I Am"

10 June 2011

I am a child of God
I am something that some can't see,
I am an image of my father
the creator who resides in me.

I am created in his image
I am a part of his will,
I am a product of his breath
in which Satan is trying to steal.

I am the opposite of a carnal mind
I am the brother of a king,
I am who I am
because of Him it's a beautiful thing.

I am victorious over my flesh
I am fasting so my spirit may eat,
I am still making this journey
because I refuse to accept defeat.

I am who He wants me to be
I am a part of His plan,
I am submissive to His power
for Him to mold me into a great man.

I am now a new creature

I am now a new born baby,

I am like a little child

from amongst sin is where He saved me.

I am now a new beginning

I am now a part of the end,

I am a stronger person

because of my new found friend.

I am a part of a larger body

I am special in every way,

I am here to serve the Lord

with faith each and every day.

I am the color of my skin

I am the hairs on my head,

I am a part of the living God

and without Him I would be dead.

I am a part of Triumph

I am a revelation of Elias D. Smith,

I am a brother to Jesus Christ

with whom I want to spend eternity with.

"An Unexpected Lesson"

4 July 2011

One night I was sitting in my cell
looking through the book of Job,
That's when I noticed a couple of things
some things that I didn't know.

Starting in chapter thirty-two
Elihu speaks his mind,
He waited for the three to stop talking
so he knew that it was his time.

He talked about a lot of things
and they really caught my attention,
So whenever I read his words
my mind had begun to listen.

He talked about how God warns his people
and he listed these three ways,
After reading them for myself
I began to think about all my days.

In a dream prophetic visions at night
when people fall into a deep sleep,
I thought about the dreams I've had
and to those warning how I didn't keep.

On their sickbeds they are disciplined
and lose their appetite for a good meal,
That's like the times that I was hospitalized
even then the warnings I ignored still.

A spokesman one in a thousand
to tell people what is right for them,
I know it meant Reverend Glover
because when I read it I thought about him.

He talked about how God was fair
and how human behavior can't change His mind,
I thought about some of my actions
and I see now that I was blind.

He talked about God's justice and ways
how they're beyond human understanding,
I then thought about some of my past
and how wrong went most of my planning.

It's amazing how God decides to teach us
whenever we're ready to know,
He taught me a valuable lesson
and I was just trying to read about Job.

It came before I finished the book
in five chapters he put me in my place,
Through the words of Elihu God spoke to me
and that really put a smile on my face.

Now about my life situations
I can't complain or say I didn't know,
Because he warned me so many times
but the right way I chose not to go.

So He allowed me to be here for a reason
so maybe His word I would no longer be missin',
It's not God's fault that I am in here
it's mine because I wouldn't listen.

We all must be born again
spiritually I must start from the beginning,
God please lead, teach, and direct me
into salvation and away from sinning.

"The Bible On Love"

30 August 2011

I know that God loves me
and I've never seen him a day in my life,
But I can't say that for the ones I know
and that cuts through me like a knife.

In the Bible it talks about love
and it says it never comes to an end,
So for the people who've said they love me
I see that's where their lies begin.

It's says that love isn't arrogant
meaning that it's not full of pride,
If a person brags about what they do for me
out of love that person has lied.

It says that love is patient
and it says that live is kind,
Then why have some said that they love me
but they've ended up leaving me behind.

It doesn't think about itself
and it doesn't keep track of wrongs,
So if I were meat burning on a grill
love would be the hand holding the tongs.

189

It says that love isn't jealous
and it doesn't sing its own praises,
Now there's something I'd have to admit
I've been guilty of that in my days.

Love never stops being patient
and it never ever gives up,
Love is like the Lord when you're thirsty
because He's always feeling your cup.

Love never stops believing
and it says it never stops hoping,
It doesn't put you down
or make you feel bad even when they are joking.

It says that love isn't rude
now I think about some of my actions,
It's been times that I have been rude
Just for my own satisfaction.

Love isn't happy with injustice
and it's always happy with the truth,
That's something Mother Holts always said
ever since the days of my youth.

"The Origin of Sin"

16 September 2011

A thought came to my mind
to write a poem again,
This time I'm going to write
on the subject of sin.

We were all born into sin
because something a man didn't do,
Even though it happened before our time
still it affects me and you.

A lot of people would say
that sin started with Adam and Eve,
But it really started before them
with an angel who didn't believe.

He didn't believe that God
was the most powerful of all,
He thought he could take his throne
and that's what caused his fall.

The most beautiful of all the angels
that beauty taken over with pride,
And because of the works of this angel
from God, Adam and Eve tried to hide.

Adam ate the forbidden fruit
at the bidding of his wife,
And from then on it ruined their chance
their chance of having eternal life.

Because Adam had sinned
the earth was cursed with death,
And in order for God to fix it
His only son had to give his last breath.

Now sin has a foundation
on earth that's where it says,
It's corrupted a lot of people
and brought them the end of their days.

The wages of sin is death
and that's something on one can deny,
Even though we were born into sin
the scriptures say that not all will die.

We all have to die once
to never ever die again,
But beware to those who die lost
and is still a slave to sin.

"Forgiveness"

11 November 2011

Forgive me for all the lies
that I've managed to tell in my life,
With them I've misled some people
and with others I've caused some strife.

Forgive me for really not listening
to things that my parents would speak,
As a child I was ignorant to a lot
and disobedience had caused me to be weak.

Forgive me for not listening to daddy
when he pleaded with me to go to college,
I thought fast money was really more important
even more important than trying to gain knowledge.

Forgive me for not obeying the commandments
even though I knew it wasn't right,
It seemed easier to yield to my flesh
to hide in darkness instead of the light.

Forgive me for the murders I've committed
regardless of what may have been the reason,
To some I just broke one of the commandments
but to others I believe it's called treason.

Forgive me for running away from home
leaving my sister and brother behind,
It was almost like I abandoned them
if I could the past I'd rewind.

Forgive me for being so selfish
and the times that I've been jealous,
I know it wasn't nothing but the devil
but me yielding caused me to be rebellious.

Forgive me for the times I'd covet
and then the times that I would steal,
Not thinking twice I'd deny my actions
and had the nerve to say that I'm real.

Forgive me for worshipping those idols
meaning the people and the worldly possessions,
Trying to get rid of my burden of sin
is what led to this poem of confessions.

Forgive me for being so arrogant
and thinking my sin was nobody's business,
I know for a fact that I've been wrong
and that's why I'm asking for your forgiveness

"If I Don't Have You"

9 December 2011

I remember why I loved them
and why I wanted to say I do,
It didn't work because I chose them
when I should have left that up to you.

I've failed at many things in life
even though I took the time to plan,
Things never worked the way that they should
because I've never took hold of your hand.

I always did believe in you
but I only had faith in myself,
Depending on the wrong things to lead me
not admitting that I needed your help.

I remember when I was in the Army
I had it made and thought I was straight,
But because I didn't have you in my life
I ended up begging you to empty my plate.

There was times when I was in the world
selling drugs and trying to be free,
That's when I got in over my head
and made it easier for Satan to harm me.

He's trying hard to take my life
and destroy the knowledge of what I've been taught,
He tried to get me to forget your promise
and how with your blood my life has been bought.

195

For as long as I can remember
you've always had my back,
And whenever I seemed to fall short
you were there to pick up the slack.

Thinking I found what I needed
in girls, cigarettes, alcohol, and weed,
I really failed to truly understand
that I need you and didn't take heed.

I hate that it took for me to end up
in jail for me to finally listen,
The whole time this could have been avoided
but it was the truth in your message I was missin'.

I'm grateful for all you've done for me
and I pray that you're not through,
Now I really know that you're all I need
and I can't succeed if I don't have you.

"If"

If someone gave you a chance
to be with whoever you wanted to be,
Would you chose to be all alone
or would you choose the trinity.

If someone gave you a key to life
and it was in the form of a book,
Would you even decide to read it
or open the cover and just have a look.

If someone had given their life
in order to take away all your wrongs,
Would you hesitate to acknowledge that person
with worship and praise through songs.

If someone really had the power
to give you peace and the power to heal,
Would you still depend on the world
or His presence would you strive to feel.

If someone would make you a promise
that you'd expect for them to keep,
Would you work to make sure it happened
or would you wait and chance falling asleep.

If someone could truly save you
from the reality of a second death,
Would you do what you could to find them
or be a victim of a spiritual theft.

If you happen to know someone
who in this poem I have described,
Then why do you have so many doubts
and behind excuses you choose to hide.

I think about the world today
and about the actions I've committed myself,
It was prophesied many times in the Bible
about certain people not wanting His help.

"My Lord"

20 December 2011

They always told me that the Lord
He's able to do anything,
No matter how big the problem
or how small He handles everything.

I'm telling you from experience
He's always been so good to me,
And even when I least expect it
He's been there to carry me.

The devil tries to knock me down
like each and every chance he gets,
But the Lord is always there
to hold me up like He aint having it.

I hope y'all really listening
Because the world is going crazy,
I gave my life to the Lord
because scriptures say that He can save me.

Now a lot of people don't understand
the joy He can bring to you inside
And know you have the respect the church
because the church is really his bride

I'm trying to tell you to praise Him
and always keep Him on your mind,
Because when it's time to be caught up
you really don't want to be left behind.

Be careful what you say in life
even if it's no one's business,
Be careful how you live your life
and always seek forgiveness.

Just know the Lord is watching
Everything you don't think He can see,
And He knows everything your thinking
even if you don't believe me.

"On Me You Can Lean"

1 May 2012

Something had started chasing him
and it was quickly starting to gain,
He ran as hard as he could
not trying to give in to worldly pain.

As he came to the end of the street
he noticed he only had two ways to go,
He looked left and then looked right
which way to take he still didn't know.

Looking left he notice the road
was as narrow as it could be,
In the distance he seen a white light
and a few people was all he could see.

To the right he'd seen in the distance
an orange glow and the road was wide,
He was shocked to see so many people
walking on while most of them cried.

While trying to make his decision
he remembered a verse and tried to picture,
In his mind what it had said
and how he'd seen it somewhere in the scriptures.

All of a sudden there appeared a man
in all white with a glowing face,
He told the boy he shouldn't stop running
and to continue to finish the race.

The boy stared at him surprised
and said he didn't know what to do,
The man looked over the boys shoulder
and said figure it out because he's coming for you.

The boy looked back then asked
what was down the road to the left with the light,
He looked the other way and shed a tear
and said to opposite of what's to the right.

He then remembered the scripture in Matthew
seven, fourteen came back to his head,
Going left he knew he would live
but going to the right he'd end up dead.

So he went down the narrow road exhausted
and caught up with the few people he'd seen,
Then the man appeared there beside him
and said if you're tired on me you can lean.

"Before It's Too Late"

26 May 2012

Sin will always keep you
longer than you want to stay,
No matter what it will always cost you
A lot more than you want to pay.

Sin shouldn't be taken lightly
as you and I both know,
Because sin will always take you
A lot further than you want to go.

Sin has a way of creeping
in and out of your life,
It will separate you from God
and cause you a lot of strife.

Sin is a real condition
into which we all were born,
That's why Christ gave his life on the cross
and it two the veil was torn.

Sin weakens the body
and puts the soul in danger,
Sin should never be comfortable
but in our lives should be as a stranger.

Sin came with a curse
affecting the earth, women, and men,
And it will always be here
until the day that Christ comes again.

Sin is the willful breaking
of religious or moral law,
This is what was committed by Adam
after the serpent showed Eve what she saw.

Sin really has a father
who is out to get you and me,
He tries to keep us in darkness
when it's God's light that we're trying to see.

With sin there's a constant battle
without Christ you can't overcome,
It will try to take a lot from you
A lot more, than more and then some.

The wages of sin is death
A price we can't afford to pay,
So change the way you think and act
and confess before it's too late.

"How To Be Free"

27 May 2012

There really is a big difference
between caution and the meaning of fear,
Like the difference sorrow and joy
and because of both you may shed a tear.

Now everything happens for a reason
and it's this that I truly do know,
I know because I've experienced
even if the reasons God didn't show.

There is something we all must do
A goal that we all must achieve,
A faith that we all must strengthen
especially in them that already believe.

Too many times I've second guessed my thoughts
not knowing what I needed to do,
The whole time the answer was in front of me
it's the Word that we know as true.

The same Word that leads and guides us
at times when we feel left behind,
The same Word that's so full of life
that when read stimulates your mind

There's so many people out there
that's on a quest for truth,
But what they fail to understand is
that the quest really starts with you.

First you have to do something
that seems to be hard for some to do,
You have to submit to the light
so the darkness can no longer blind you.

Second you have to understand
and you truly have to believe,
That you were bought with a price
that no mind or computer can truly conceive.

Third you have to confess your sins and
ask for forgiveness to be exempt from the fire,
But if you claim to not have any at all
then it's you the scriptures do call a liar.

After this you are truly free
from what's called the bondage of sin,
And for guidance you must study the scriptures
for this long journey you're about to begin.

"Add To Your Faith"

24 June 2012

To this you must add that
and to that you must add this,
Take heed to the words of this poem
because ignorance really isn't bliss.

In the second letter of Peter
it says to faith we are to add integrity,
Meaning even when no one is watching
we are to be true which can add longevity.

Now again still in verse five
it says to integrity we are to add knowledge,
Meaning knowledge of the word of God
not any wisdom you attain from a college.

Then to knowledge we are to add temperance
which is another word for self-control,
Now for some it really is needed
so for them it becomes a main goal.

Then to temperance we are to add patience
and that's something I truly do need,
Right now it's what I'm being taught
and it's a struggle believe you me.

Then to patience we are to add godliness
Meaning to God we are to be more devout,
Believe me that's something that's needed
because it's Him that we can't do without.

Then to godliness we're to add brotherly kindness
in other words add Christian affection,
Love your neighbor as you love thy self
that command in itself is a blessin'.

Then to brotherly kindness we're to add charity
which is also another word for love,
Now that's something even when we don't deserve it
that we receive from our God above.

Scriptures say if you have these qualities
and if in you they are increasing,
Then your knowledge about our Lord Jesus Christ
is productive and never depleting.

But if these qualities aren't present in your life
then you're short sighted and truly forgotten,
That you were cleansed from your past sins
by the blood of Gods only begotten.

"Books Of The Bible"

24 June 2012

Genesis, Exodus, Leviticus
Numbers and then Deuteronomy,
The first five books of the bible
the one sitting right here in front of me.

Joshua, Judges, and Ruth
Samuel, Kings, and Chronicles,
Ezra then Nehemiah
and then Esther who was phenomenal.

Job, Psalms, Proverbs
Ecclesiastes and Song of Songs,
These are the books of wisdom
so with these you can't go wrong.

Isaiah, Jeremiah, Lamentations
Ezekiel and the good old Daniel,
With God's help there wasn't a problem
or situation that he couldn't handle.

Hosea, Joel, and Amos
Obadiah then that man Jonah,
He was put in the belly of a whale
after he told God that he didn't wonna.

Micah, Nahum, Habakkuk
Zephaniah, and the Haggai,
These are the book of the prophets
that ends with Zechariah and Malachi.

Then there's the books of the gospels
that tells about the son from above,
Matthew, Mark, Luke then John
the disciples whom Jesus did love.

Then it's the book of the history
of the church and all of its facts,
In which tells the story of Saul
who became Paul and all of his Acts.

Then you have Romans, Corinthians, Galatians
Ephesians, Philippians, Colossians,
The first six books of the letters
full of encouragement and full of cautions.

Thessalonians, Timothy, Titus
Philemon, Hebrews, and James,
Peter, the Johns, and Jude
then Revelation ends the game.

Chapter 6

REFLECTIONS

R.I.P.

"You All I'll Keep Close"

20 July 2003

I often think about
and wonder why,
The ones we love
seem like the first to die.

Pray for me y'all
because I'm losing my head
My only grandfather
has been pronounced dead.

I really do miss him
and I know that you do too,
He was the first member
of our little Holts crew.

Daddy Bill was cool
and you know he was wild,
I'd laugh when I'd see him
play with his youngest grandchild.

The longer I sit
the more I begin to thinking,
And I see his face
every time when I blink.

I miss him so much
that I really can't explain,
I really don't need to
because I'm sure you can see my pain.

I try to hide it
but that I can't do,
What makes me feel better
is hanging with my crew.

I thank them for all
the support they've given me,
If I need something to cry on
that shoulder they would be.

It's good to have friends
especially ones like mine,
That can make me laugh
and feel good all the time.

For my friends and family
I say to you be safe,
You never know what could happen
at any time or any day.

So I'll end this poem
on a serious note
I really do love you all
and you all I'll keep close.

"Daddy Bill"

20 July 2003

For the ones that knew
him as Daddy Bill,
Then it is my pain
that you can truly feel.

I'm going to miss Daddy Bill
for the rest of my life,
It might have been his time to go
but I feel that it wasn't right.

I really miss his presence
and I really miss his voice,
I even miss hearing him yell
after I've made a bad choice.

He used to ask me a
about his old Chevy,
And about the same car
he'd yell and then ask heavy.

Daddy Bill was really a trip
and that I'll never forget,
He'd get real mad at times
and then start talking shit.

He used to take trips
up and down the road,
Me and my sister Angel
would always want to go.

Sometimes he would take us
and then sometimes he wouldn't,
Sometimes he didn't take us
because he knew that he shouldn't.

I know that I'll really
truly miss that man,
And I really wished
that he was God's own man.

When something goes bad
I'm going to just keep it real,
And say "hot damn"
Just like Daddy Bill.

IN MEMORY
OF
WILLIAM HOLTS

DECEMBER 21, 1921 – JULY 19,2003

Saturday, July 26,2003

1:00 P.M.

Johnson Funeral Home

Lynch, Kentuky

"A Sad Day"

Today is your birthday
and I wish you were really here,
Instead of me celebrating
I just sit and shed a tear.

You're my only son
even though you're not living,
I lost you four years ago
right before thanksgiving.

Today I'm supposed to celebrate
but I can't do it without you,
I get angry and then I cry
because I'm hurting it's true.

I pray and I ask
for God to bring me another,
But the answer to my prayers
seem to go straight to my brother.

I miss you so much
and that I really do,
I lost my first born
and he was only two.

How do you laugh
when someone has fallen,
The same way you awe
when a baby starts walkin'.

How do you feel
when everything hits the fan,
The same way you do
when she ruins that perfect plan.

I love you my son
if you listening you'll know it's true,
And I know that God
will always take care of you.

"Missing You"

24 June 2004

Waking up—everyday—thinking about—many things
Me and you—growing up—growing up—chillin' man.

Don't understand—the reason why—that man took—your life away
When I heard—couldn't cry—hit my knees—then I prayed

I asked God—to please—let you walk—through the door
Opened my eyes—didn't see you—closed them back—prayed some more

Can't believe—you are gone—and you're never—coming back
Help me Lord—help me now—before I end—up on my back.

Miss him man—love him man—always—he was my friend
He'd always ride—no matter what—'til the very—very end.

My hearts heavy—my minds gone—but I try to—stay strong
I've noticed that—it's hard to do—even if—I am grown.

Feeling bad—feeling sad—always—feeling pain
Still don't—understand—why he took—my friend away.

Little Rut—wanting you—right here—with me
Hurts when—you're not there—chilling on—first street.

[Hook] (2x)
We be missing you
W-e b-e miss-ing you
We be missing you
W-e b-e miss-ing you

"Missing You" (verse 2)

10 o'clock—Saturday—morning my—phone rings
It was Tonya—talking 'bout—I think you need to—take a seat.

Daddy Bill—went away—and he's never—coming back
Said he died—earlier—of a massive—heart attack.

Daddy Bill—I miss you man—and you know—you know it's true
I never pictured—waking up—waking up—not seeing you.

It seems like—the ones we love—are the first—the first to die
Don't think about it—to much—but when I do—I start to cry.

I try to hide—my feelings man—but I can't—do it alone
Breaking down—every time—every time—I go back home.

The pain I feel—I can't explain—but it tries—to take me man
Off the edge—can you feel me—do you really—feel my pain.

Need some guidance—need some hope—Lord please—don't let me go
Need your strength—everyday—so I can keep—holding on.

I miss you daddy—I really do—I'm a keep—my mind strong
Still gonna—talk to you—even though—you're not at home.

[Hook] (2x)
We be missing
W-e b-e miss-ing you
Wc bc missing
W-e b-e miss-ing you

"Missing You" (verse 3)

Even though—you don't know—any names—on this track
They really mean—the world to me—and I wish—I had them back.

This is for—anybody—that's ever lost—anyone
By accident—natural cause-even if—by the gun.

Don't hold—your feelings back—let them loose—let them flow
Remember that-everybody's—got a time—when they go.

You may not—feel my pain—and that goes—both ways
But I know—that we all—are wishing for—better days.

Daddy Bill—Big Vay—Little Rut—Larry too
To me they really—are alive—even though it—aint the truth.

Memories—hold them close—try to never—let them go
I'm serious—when I say—when I say—life is short.

Everything—happens for a—reason even—if we don't
Understand—what it is—don't contemplate—let it go.

You shouldn't live—in the past—cause its all—in your head
I know its true—but I can't—forget about—the ones that dead.

[Hook] (2x)
We be missing you
W-e b-e miss—ing you
We be missing you
W-e b-e miss-ing you

"A Mournful Day"

24 November 2005

When I woke up this morning
I felt a little strange,
And a little out of place
but not at all any pain.

I tried all day
to keep a smile on my face,
Which I found hard to do
when it's a day like today.

I haven't talked to anyone
I'm trying to keep it inside,
But regardless of what I do
my feeling I cannot hide.

Six years ago today
I lost something of mine,
I am not yet over it
but I know it will take time.

I miss my little boy
and love him I really do,
I think about him everyday
man! He was only two.

A secret never told
until that secret passed away,
A life never lived
until another died one day.

"Katherleen Newman"

26 May 2009

Knowing at all times

And understanding the choice she made

That if she put her faith in God

He'd always show her the way

Eternal life is what she was

Relieve from worldly pain

Light from the son is all she'll see

Everything hard now simple and plain

Every time that she would preach

New lessons you learned about life

No matter what it always

Every truth cutting through like a knife

We'll always miss her presence

Mother Newman would always plead

Always put your faith in God

No matter what He's all you need

"I Remember"

5 July 2011

I remember like yesterday
the good times we used to have,
I remember how you would pick with your sister
and how much it would make me laugh.

I remember in upward bound
how funny I realized you was,
At your request I'd stay in your room
I was proud to call you my cuz.

I remember the time when I ordered pizza
and how you almost ate a whole box,
You ended up being so full
it almost hurt to put on your socks.

I remember when you would say
grab a pen and let's write some rhymes,
When I'd say that I couldn't write
you'd look at me and say quit lyin'.

I remember when I'd hear you rap
I would yell "go Bowser go",
You'd smile and look right in my face
and say boy they just don't know.

I remember the day I heard
the day I heard that you had died,
I really couldn't believe it
I just sat in my cell and cried.

I'll remember you for the rest of my life
and you know that I always will,
No matter what we'll always be family
and in my heart we'll always chill.

Bowser I'll always love you
and I believe you know it's true,
Right now you're somewhere special
and God will always take care of you.

"My Uncle Ray"

14 April 20112

He was a grandfather to some
and an uncle to others,
He was a father of daughters
and a father of brothers.

He knew you couldn't find truth
with an ax or a drill,
By living in a big house
or in a mine full of steel.

He seen through a lot of smiles
and smelt truth in the distance,
He knew true happiness was not easy
for a middle class existence.

And aint no way anyone
could ever play him out,
Because he always represented the present
he represented the right now.

Another frame of mind
existing beyond comprehension,
He may not have been perfect
but did his best with good intentions.

Strong willed all his life
steadily fighting without end,
Endless nights, kicks, and fights
against time and all its friends.

His wife was there to the end
not once without emotion,
There's nothing more inviolate
or greater than a wife's devotion.

I just wish I could have been there
before he took his last breath,
To at least say goodbye
to my Uncle Ray before his death.

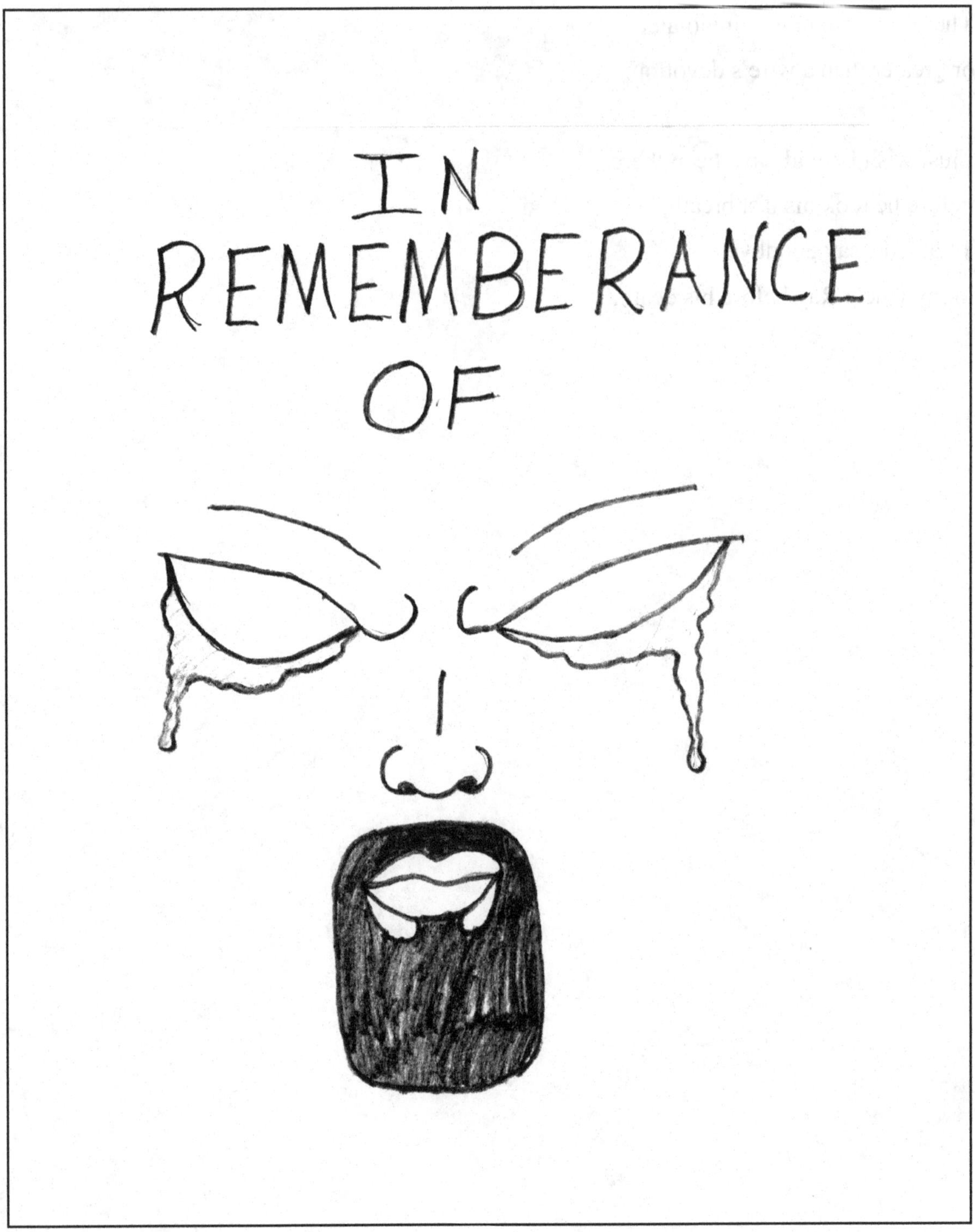
IN
REMEMBERANCE
OF

IN REMEMBRANCE OF

Rutland "Lil Rut" Melton
7-31-80 to 5-12-02

Markelle Pettygrue
1-25-76 to 1-12-08

Larry "Bubba" Jones
8-29-80 to 8-22-03

Johnny Pettygrue
3-19-13 to 11-12-04

Rev. Katherleen Newman
11-24-10 to 5-25-09

William "Baby Ray" Cook
9-18-25 to 4-12-12

Jamal "Lil Crow" Covington
12-11-79 to 4-20-05

David Demonte Spencer
11-247-96 to 11-21-99

McKinley "Bowser" Dunson
2-9-91 to 6-23-11

Seale "Champ" Baskin
7-28-76 to 4-12-03

Zelpha "Kojak" Warren
8-19-80 to 4-17-05

Latasa "Tasa" Kirk
4-20-84 to 4-20-05

William "Wild Bill" Holts Sr.
12-21-21 to 7-29-03

Lottie Pettygrue
3-17-18 to 1-15-11

Jay Feltner
5-27-89 to 7-15-11

Troy Davis
10-9-68 to 9-21-11

Gilbert Holts Sr. lives in the Southern United States. He's been writing poetry for about twelve years and this is his first book.